SEND HELP...
and coffee!

WRITTEN BY
Amy Mykytiuk

Stones in Clay
PUBLISHING

A SHOT OF ENCOURAGEMENT FOR HOME SCHOOL MOMS

Send Help … and Coffee!

Stones in Clay Publishing
P.O. Box 1302
Newcastle, Ok 73065

> *Living Stones, being built up as a spiritual house for a holy priesthood, to offer up spiritual sacrifices acceptable to God through Jesus Christ. . . 1 Peter 2:5*
>
> *But we have this treasure in jars of clay, to show that the surpassing power belongs to God and not to us.*
>
> *1 Corinthians 4:7*

Cover Design by Mindi Stucks
Illustrated by the Mykytiuk children

Published in United States of America
ISBN 978-0-9989522-4-6
Christian/Family/Parenting/Education
2018.5.31

Stones in Clay
PUBLISHING

Forward

You will be encouraged as I was by her honesty, relatable life, hilarious stories, and each touching prayer at the end of the devotionals that just make you feel loved and accepted right where you are in life.

If I know my friend, Amy, this was the point all along, to help us Mom's realize that no matter where we are in life, whatever level of crazy we find ourselves, we need to be there for one another. Praying, encouraging, crying, laughing, loving, and accepting each other as Christ has accepted us.

This is what Amy has done for me and my prayer for you is that you see her heart in her words and find some extra encouragement for today.

Deonna Linsky
Homeschool mom of five girls

Find Your Tribe

AS MOMS, I really don't think we give ourselves enough credit. The world goes out of their way to recognize mothers and the significant role they play in the lives of their children and family, but as mothers, we sell ourselves short. There is a divine element to being a mother that no one else can truly understand, except other mothers.

I believe this holds true in different communities of mothers as well.

Homeschooling moms understand the stress of the responsibility they have accepted in their children's education that moms of public school kids never experience in the same way and vice versa. The working mothers understand the pressure to make ends meet and care for a home in a way no stay-at-home mother can. The same is true of stay at home moms, moms of big families, moms that struggled with infertility, empty nest moms, single moms, adoptive moms, foster moms, sports moms, dance moms, music moms, moms that have lost a child, moms of special needs kids… the list really could go on and on. We all have our tribe or tribes, and they just "get us" like no one else, simply because they've been there too.

I am a homeschooling mother of five kids. Some consider me a mother of a large family, and others, not so much. I am a mother to teenage boys, one grade school boy, and a mother to just one girl. I am a stay-at-home "working" mother that works some from home to help with income. I'm a crunchy mother. I'm a loud, boisterous, often mouthy mother that sometimes yells. In fact, I am always amazed and in awe of the quiet gentle mothers I come across and how quiet and gentle their children tend to be. They usually can't handle too much of our family. I am drawn to the mothers who clearly do not have it all together and tend to shy away from the ones who seem to have it all figured out.

Even though most of my tribe consists of mothers like me, before I am a mother, I am more importantly a wife. In fact, I am a pastor's wife. That tribe is quite small and exclusive. I do not thrive in exclusivity, but rather inclusivity, so this role is a constant challenge in my life.

Those two titles, wife and mother, encompass so much about who I am, what

I do, what I endure, the burden I carry, and the abundance with which I am blessed. Those roles are primary, dictate all my other activities, and consume all my time, energy and mind. However, I am one thing more than both of those put together; I am a follower of Jesus, of the One and only True God, and the King of Kings. Best of all, He is my Father, parenting and loving me, calling me daughter. Because of this, I have hope on the dark days and the days I feel defeated. Because of Jesus, I know that even when my heart and mind and body are too weary to move or fathom how I will ever manage to raise my children and finish well, I lean into Him, find my refuge and rest and strength in Him, and push forward, because, sweet Mama, our labor is not in vain.

"Therefore, my beloved [sisters], be steadfast immovable, always abounding in the work of the Lord, knowing that in the Lord your labor is not in vain." 1 Corinthians. 15:58

Trouble Will Come;
Bring On the Coffee!

EATING PASSOVER DINNER with his closest friends, Jesus informed the disciples that He would be leaving them soon. Of course they didn't like hearing their Lord was going away, and by going away, they had no idea what He truly meant, but He did promise to send a Helper to them to fill his place. Jesus also explained that though they would go through a time of sadness, in the end, they would be reunited and rejoice.

So also you have sorrow now, but I will see you again, and your hearts will rejoice, and no one will take your joy from you. John 16:22

Notice that Jesus did not promise to take away their sorrow. He promised the sorrow would end with rejoicing.

As the night wore on, Jesus finished off with a promise, *I have said these things to you, that in me you may have peace. In the world you will have tribulation. John 16:33a*

He promised that in this world we will have trouble, trials, suffering, difficulties or tribulation. That promise never brings me comfort except when the trouble comes I know Jesus said it would, therefore there is no surprise at its arrival. However, Jesus used one little word that brought hope, "BUT!" The word says, although there might be suffering, we are not defeated. We are not overcome. We are not destroyed. Jesus declared victory with that one little word before He became the victor because He knew the end of the story.

"But, take heart; I have *overcome* the world."

Jesus didn't say, I will overcome. He said, I have overcome. Before his death and resurrection, Jesus had already conquered the tribulation, the difficulty, the pain, the sorrow, the obstacle, the exhaustion, the sickness, and the suffering. He knew what waited at the end: rejoicing and a joy that cannot be taken away.

Jay and I have seen our fair share of trouble in this world. Some of it came because of our own mistakes and some of it resulted from living on planet earth. We've had marriage troubles that nearly tore us apart. I realize it is only by the grace of God we made it through the first year of marriage, and honestly, it is only by the grace of God and our reliance on Him that we make it every single year since. We are humans with many, many flaws.

We have experienced trouble with work and jobs. Friendships have suffered, and we have had good friends that we have lost. We've had trouble with family and church, our kids, health, and we've even had trouble with finances.

The truth is, we all have trouble in all areas of our life. The people with the most money can't buy their troubles a one-way ticket to Antarctica any more than those that make the least amount of money. Pastoring and serving in the ministry doesn't take away from the amount of troubles pastors and ministers and missionaries experience. There is no plastic bubble for anyone to live in which will protect them from all the troubles in the world. Everyone that breathes and calls themselves human, has trouble.

BUT!

That one little word indicates there is hope, and there is a way to overcome even when it seems hopeless. Robert Frost wrote in his poem, "A Servant of Servants,"

Len says one steady pull more ought to do it. He says the best way out is always through. And I agree to that, or in so far As that I can see no way out but through—Leastways for me—and then they'll be convinced. (ll. 55-59)

Sometimes, the only way out, is through. While Jesus never indicated that He will save us from the trouble, or take the trouble away, He does give us the way through the trouble. He is the way through. He is the victor, and we need to realize without a good shot of Jesus every day, there is no way we can do it all.

The most beautiful message Jesus gave his disciples at this point, when they had no idea what kind of trouble they would face, begins with the image of a mother.

"When a woman is giving birth, she has sorrow because *her hour has come*, but when she has delivered the baby, she no longer remembers the anguish, for joy that a human being has been born into the world. So also you have sorrow now, but I will see you again and your hearts will rejoice, and no one will take your joy from you." John 16:21-22

I remember the first time I gave birth. I could not see or hear a thing through the pain. Sorrow is far too mild of a word to describe the 26 hours of labor and delivery I experienced. I even said, "I will never forget the pain, I'm not sure I'll be willing to do it again."

However, it wasn't long until I could no longer remember the morning sickness, the pressure on my back and hips as I tried to carry a growing human being, or recall even the intense labor and birth of my baby. The joy my little boy gave me far outweighed the pain and sorrow. I wanted to do it again, to suffer through every step so that I might increase my joy!

While we might not face persecution like the disciples did as we educate our offspring, we face days which will try us in every way possible, and some days we might ask, "Why, Lord, did you think I could be a good mother to these children?" Some days there isn't enough coffee or enough patience or enough yelling or rules. However, there is always enough Jesus, and He hears your pleas for help, and He's already there. In the darkness, when you can't see, He has given us Himself, the victor, to overcome the troubles.

Sometimes the trouble comes from outside the home, and that makes our primary job to educate our children more difficult. Kids don't understand the stress of money or jobs and adult life. Sometimes moms get sick for a couple of days, and sometimes moms suffer with chronic illness. Those kinds of troubles can make simply living and breathing impossible, not to mention caring for a home and family. Homeschooling feels utterly impossible. Some of those troubles can make living feel impossible.

My prayer for you as I write this is the words of this book can offer encouragement in your difficult days. I pray you experience Jesus as He comes to your rescue through His Word on the difficult days and the difficult seasons. I pray, as you walk this journey with me, you will hold on to the promise. In the end, there will be much to rejoice over and even more, no circumstance and no person can steal the joy Jesus has brought you.

May your coffee be strong,
your patience be long,
and your kids choose right
over wrong.

Who I Am

SOME MORNINGS.... I forget who I am. Who am I kidding? **MOST** mornings, I forget that of all my titles, I am most importantly a daughter of God. How incredible He gives me the title, along with his deep, intimate, divine love which exceeds any love this world can offer.

Nope. I wake up thinking about my day of lessons and cleaning and laundry and cooking or errands. My list is long, and it rarely includes fully engaging in my role as a daughter of THE King! Yet, without spending time first in my role as a child of God, all of my other roles suffer.

That's the hard part. I may take some time while I shower or make my coffee to lift up my requests, but to spend meaningful and purposeful time in His presence seems impossible on most days. On most days, if I don't hit the floor running, I tend to hide under the covers, mustering the courage to face all my many responsibilities and to-do list.

Even more, if I find some time apart from all the hub-bub of my household, I seldom stay there for a long period of time, at least not without an interruption every three minutes. I promise you, I can waste hours on the internet without ever hearing a peep from one of my kids, but if the pages of my Bible make even a small hint of noise, the entire house turns into chaos and madness.

There. I've said it and now you can judge me or become my best friend, but I am a pastor's wife, homeschooling mom that struggles to spend a designated period of time alone with my Bible and prayer journal every day. Before you ask, my husband knows this, and loves me anyway.

On a daily basis I find myself at a point where I send up an SOS, "Send Help!" Fortunately for me help is always waiting on my end table, in the pages of my well-loved, worn out Bible, if I'll just take a moment to open it up and enjoy it with a good cup of coffee.

Messing Up

I AM EIGHTEEN years into this beautiful thing called marriage. Seventeen years into parenthood, and finishing my 9th year in homeschooling. With all my years of experience, I still mess it up on a daily basis, and if most people are honest, they know I'm not

Scripture is relevant in all of our lives

alone. This devotional crosses into all the tribes because one thing is for sure: scripture is relevant in all of our lives and situations, and this is my attempt to get it right by seeking answers in scripture on a daily basis. I am taking the challenge to look at my life through the lenses of scripture every day when I do school with my kids. I'm taking you along for the journey, because we are of the same tribe, sisters in Christ. I'm sure you will see me completely drop the ball, and hopefully you will nod in agreement with me as I confess my failures. I pray for you, as you face the messy days of life too. Most of all I hope my journey will encourage you on your own journey, to lift your spirits, encourage you to keep going, comfort you through the tough days, and give you more reasons to rejoice, laugh, and give thanks.

Rejoice
Laugh
Give Thanks

Prove It

Every word of God is tested, He is a shield to those who take refuge in Him. Proverbs 30:5

LIFE IS OFTEN divided up into before and after. There are moments that define us and dictate which direction our life will take. We talk about events in terms of before said event or after. I never realized this until I went to lunch with a couple who had lost their youngest forever. As they recalled some event in their life, Dad asked, "Was that before Jack or after?"

Sometimes it can be a good thing, like a wedding or the birth of a child, but often it is the tragedies that divide our lives into parts.

I became a follower of Jesus Christ when I was ten years-old, after one major event changed and divided my life forever.

At the age of nine, I asked my mother many questions about God and salvation. I was waiting on that moment to receive a "call" to be saved. I felt as though the time was slipping away, and God hadn't made any effort to call me, so I began to doubt Him. Science interested me, and as I learned more about evolution I questioned the validity of this story I had been taught about God and Jesus. I can still remember at the age of two or three thinking the story of Santa Clause was completely ridiculous. However, the story of Jesus, had never raised questions of validity in my nine years of life.

I asked myself, "If evolution is true, and science can prove all this, then how can I believe in God? How can I know this isn't something someone just made up at some time?"

Frustrated with all my doubts, I began to pray and ask for an answer, skeptical that I would ever receive one. My prayer went like this, "God, if you're real, prove it to me with a miracle. I don't mean a small miracle that I can doubt or someone could disprove, but something big. I want to see someone healed or brought back to life, or a bunch of people fed with just a little bit of food, just like in the Bible. I want there to be no doubt in my mind and my heart, it was You that performed a miracle."

A couple of weeks later I fell under a brush hog, or a large shredder that is pulled behind a tractor. We lived on five acres, and we used the brush hog to "mow" our acreage. It was attached to an old tractor that was so old we started it with a crank in the front.

I sat on the fender of the wheel of that tractor and rode along with my fourteen-year-old step-brother, Josh, as he finished up the last of the yard. My mother thought he had finished mowing, so she allowed me to ride with him since the brush hog turned off. However, he decided to finish a small patch around a tree.

As I rode along, I stared down at the mover drive shaft spinning at lightning speed and remembered all the warnings my grandfather had given me about that brush hog and tractor. There's no way I could survive if I fell down there. "That'll never happen to me, I thought."

That'll never happen to me!

As he drove around the tree, I raised my hand to push a branch out of the way as I had done many times before, but this branch didn't budge. It pushed me off the tractor.

The next few seconds seemed to last forever as life moved in slow motion. I watched the ground move closer as I heard Josh scream my name. Responding to his call, I spun in mid-air, preventing me from falling under the brush hog head first.

It was as if I was seeing life in still moments and had no control over my actions at the same time. I realized I was clawing at the ground and screaming, but I felt nothing. My thoughts turned to the lack of pain I felt as I convinced myself, "It missed me! I don't feel anything. It must've missed me."

Because of my grandfather, a life-long farmer, and all his lectures on the dangers of a brush hog, I was not ignorant of the damage it could do. We knew farmers whose legs had become stuck in farm equipment like combines. I knew it would cut me to pieces, but I felt nothing. So it must've missed me, or so I thought.

Josh, having shut down the tractor and jumped off, panicked and stood next to the brush hog and me as I turned my body over to see what happened. At that moment, Josh scooped me in his arms and began running to the house. I reached down to feel my leg only to take hold of bone. It was at that moment I knew it hadn't missed me.

Over the next month I underwent so many surgeries we lost count. I kept my leg, but I lost my Achilles tendon. I would most definitely be crippled for life, but I was alive, and that in itself was a miracle. We heard story after story of a child that died under a brush hog. Never did we hear a story of one surviving.

The massive blades never touched even one of my arteries, the first miracle that saved my life, although they did cut away my entire right calf, Achilles tendon, heel, part of my left heel, and sliced open my right thigh from my hip to my knee all the way to the femur. The blades never touched a joint either, another miracle, leaving all bones in tact except my heel, which the doctors had carefully placed together as best they could.

After weeks of skin grafts, and hundreds of stitches and staples, the main issue I faced was my Achilles tendon. It was gone for good, and tendons don't grow back.

But.

There's that word, the one which scripture uses to show how in the midst of the darkest night, there is hope, and God is about to step in and change everything for good. God had so much good in store for me.

The Impossible
Becomes the Possible

THAT'S ALWAYS THE most beautiful part of a story. *But God.* He changes the impossible to possible and the sorrow to joy. He changes a tragedy to a victory and heals what is broken, making it whole again.

My Achilles tendon was gone, and my doctor needed to fuse my ankle so the rest of my muscles wouldn't atrophy, but my mother felt like it was too permanent and too drastic. She wanted to see me healed, not welded and pieced back together. In her sorrow, she prayed, *"This is more than I can bear. This is the miracle child you gave me. You promised . . . God please heal her."* As soon as she said her prayer, I yelled for her to come see.

I had not been able to move my foot since the accident, but that hadn't stopped my mom from encouraging me to exercise it daily. I pulled my foot toward my body using my hand, and miraculously pushed it to a pointing position without any help from anything except the new Achilles tendon God had placed in my leg!

When we went back to visit the doctor, and he saw me move my foot unassisted, with a brand new tendon flexing, his jaw dropped. He had no explanation and nothing left to do to me, so he released me.

At the tender age of ten, I had no idea what happened in my body, but my mother, a former nursing student, understood fully. She explained to me that my tendon was gone, and now it was back. She explained no part of our body, not even tendons, can grow back. When they are gone, they are gone forever. She told me how she prayed and in that moment, I began to move my foot again, indicating a tendon had grown back, miraculously.

At that moment the light bulb went on in my head. I remembered my prayer, and I knew immediately God had answered my

God answered my prayer

prayer and given me my miracle. I knew without a doubt in my mind He is not only real, but actively, lovingly pursing me.

Exactly one year after my accident, I was baptized, declaring my adoption into the family of God as his daughter. He took me broken and made me whole. He took my doubts and turned them to rock, solid faith.

I made a promise to Him that every time someone asked about my scars, which cover all of my right side, I would not tell them about my accident without telling them how God saved me from death, healed me, and then saved me again, but this time, from eternal death.

God's Prosperity

MY MOTHER WORRIED about me growing up with so many scars, just as any mother would do for her daughter. She worried that other girls might make fun of me. They did. She worried I might be rejected, looked over, or ignored by boys. I'm sure I was, unbeknownst to me. She was worried people would stare. They do. She was worried my self-image would be damaged. Never. Not even a little, because while people see scars on my body, I see the fingerprints of God. I see He touched me in a way He has touched few people, and He gave me a testimony I can't deny. His love is written all over me in a way many will never experience. It doesn't hurt my self-image to look imperfect, and I don't have to pretend to be perfect, but instead, these imperfections, flaws and scars destroy my self-esteem and give me back a confidence in the only One who can fix every single one of them, because I have proof beyond proof, not only does God exist, He hears me. He answers me, and He loves me, scars, flaws, and all.

The thing I love most is the Bible teaches us He didn't just choose to mark me to show me how much He loves just *me*. He loves us all the same, and I am a walking testimony to just how great His love is. He is willing to go to any length to show all of us and to welcome us home.

My scars are not just a reminder for me that God is real, any more than Lazarus' resurrection was just for him to be able to live again, or the blind man's sight is just for him to see again, or Joseph's dreams were just for him to know the future, or Elijah's drenching, wet sacrifice was just for him to prove God is more powerful than the prophets of Baal. They are all God's acts on, and in, our lives to bring glory to Himself, to be a testimony to everyone that hears and everyone that sees, so that beyond any doubt, people will know He alone is God, and He alone can do the miraculous.

While the question may linger, why did this happen to me God, why must I be so hard-headed that you need to prove yourself to me in such a dramatic way, I've always found the answer in Jeremiah 29:11.

For I know the plans I have for you, declares the Lord, plans to prosper you and not to harm you, plans to give you a hope and a future. Jeremiah 29:11

Whatever God allows in my life, I know without a doubt, it is ultimately for my good. It's much easier to understand as a parent, temporal comfort is not nearly as important as my eternal residence or my character. As parents we allow difficulties to come into our children's lives, sometimes it causes them pain for their ultimate good. A good example is removing a splinter from a kid's foot. The only thing equal to such a task is wrestling an alligator under water. Digging that splinter out may cause that child discomfort and even pain but without removing it from their flesh they will experience even more pain and possible infection that left untreated could lead to some serious health problems, even amputation. God allowed a small amount of pain and discomfort in my life here on earth so that I might be with Him for eternity.

In a verse in the book of Jeremiah, God isn't speaking of prosperity in monetary terms, but rather in Kingdom terms. He wants to prosper us in our relationship to Him and with others. Everything else is temporal and meaningless.

Even in what seemed like the hardest, darkest hours of my life, this verse stuck out to me, accompanied with a picture which said, "The best is yet to come."

Giving in to His will, His plan, and His way brings the absolute best outcome, a closer relationship with Himself.

More on that later. Right now, I want you to think and ask yourself what the fingerprints of God are on your own life. They may not appear physically on your body as mine do. They may appear in your healed marriage, your miraculous funds that never work out on paper but seem to be just enough each month, or your kids' lives, your own heart, or within the healing of your mind. Whatever it is, they are there, screaming to the world, *Praise God! He alone is worthy of our praise!*

Beautiful Scars

DO YOU HIDE your scars from the world, worried that people will make fun of you? I guarantee they will. Do you hide your flaws, worried people will reject you, stare at you, or call you weird? They most definitely will. I can promise however, that displaying those scars for the world to see will also give you an opportunity to honor God in a way you could never imagine.

Likewise, what are some of the fingerprints God is leaving on your children, and are you trying to cover those so the world can't see? Let your children's scars show too! Teach them to use those flaws for God's glory!

Take some time to thank God for the difficult situations you and your family have encountered in the past and the ones you are in now, and reflect on some of the people in the Bible mentioned here and the difficulties God used to bring glory to His Name. Ask Him to give you excitement as you look forward to how He will be glorified in the midst of your daily trial to raise unruly children into Godly adults!

One of my biggest pet peeves is when people hear my story and say something along the lines of "Oh my goodness. I could never go through something like that." Or "You are so strong."

I'm not strong at all, I start over every morning

My first thought is, "No, I'm really not strong at all, but what choice do I have?" I still deal with my injury on a daily basis.

In fact, as we speak I am laid up on the couch hoping an incision from a surgery four months ago will heal up. I have poor circulation in my foot and healing is a long, frustrating process. I deal with pain almost daily. Before this surgery, the longest I ever went without surgery, was six years.

It's a daily battle, and even my husband will throw out the "You're so strong" comment. It enrages me. I'm not strong. I never feel strong. I feel weak and broken most of the time. People see an injured woman still going strong. I am going strong, and I thank God for every day I can still get up and be active. However, the fact still remains, this wasn't a choice for me. I can get up and go each morning, using the body God gave me, the situation He has me in, or what? Quit? I have felt like quitting many times, but that's not an option. That's not how a daughter of the King behaves. That's not what Jesus taught His disciples to do.

While I sit on the couch, frustrated at the effort it takes to just go to the bathroom, or get a drink of water, I push forward. Right now the kids are not going on amazing field trips, pursuing elaborate experiments, or even studying much more than the bare bones, basics, and that's okay. Some seasons require less work, and more reliance on the Lord for his grace to sustain us and push us through. This is one of those times.

Honestly, I have more days I lay down and cry, than days I stand up on my one good foot and straighten my crown. Even in those times His grace sustains me, picks me up, pushes me through, gives me the ability to ignore the dirty house and continue on with my responsibilities. His grace says, it's okay to sleep and allow your body to heal. It does not make you a failure as a mom to be broken sometimes. We are all broken at some point. That's when we experience His grace more abundantly.

If there is one thing I could tell everyone, it would be that it's not my strength or my stubbornness, as great as it may be, that keeps me going day after day. Nope. It's God's grace, plain and simple.

Promise

"But He said to me, 'My grace is sufficient for you, for my power is made perfect in weakness.' Therefore, I will boast all the more gladly of my weaknesses, so that the power of Christ may rest upon me. For the sake of Christ, then, I am content with weaknesses, insults, hardships, persecutions, and calamities. For when I am weak, then I am strong." 2 Corinthians 12:9-10

God's grace is sufficient in even the unimaginable difficult days.

JUST LAST WEEK my best friend's grandson was diagnosed with a tumor. I drove to the hospital to be with the family, and I watched this Mama. She babysat our kids when she was just a young teenager. My husband officiated her wedding, and I was her doula for this baby boy's birth. I watched this Mama, so tired and broken, just days after being told her sweet little baby had a tumor that covers three-fourths of his liver, smile and hold and care for him like only a mother could.

I had to look away so many times and dry the tears in my eyes, but one time I forced myself to look and feel the full weight of the situation. I cried out in my heart, "Oh God. I could never hold it together like she is!"

I couldn't. That's the truth, because He is not strengthening me for that journey, He is strengthening her. It is not my burden as a mother, so the grace is not given to me, but His grace is more than sufficient for her, just as it has been sufficient for me through all my trials as a mother.

Every day, as mothers, we face difficulties and trials and burdens, but God promises He has a portion to give us every single second of the day, to strengthen us for everything from a boo-boo, to the absolute unimaginable. His grace is sufficient. His joy is my strength.

> *The LORD is my strength and my shield;*
> *My heart trusts in Him, and I am helped;*
> *Therefore my heart exults,*
> *And with my song I shall thank Him.*
> *Psalm 28:7*

Thankfulness

MY MOTHER NEVER forgave herself after my accident. While she can discuss it, she can't discuss it with the same joy and celebration I can. I will always retell my story as the best thing that ever happened to me because it introduced me to Jesus.

If I could go back, I'd do it all exactly the same, except I might be nicer to my mother when it came to picking out my shoes. (She added that last statement.)

I thank God for my accident and for the trials it put me through. I thank God for the stares I felt as I swam at the pool because they taught me to ignore rude people and to use my differences to open a meaningful conversation with others. I thank God for the rude comments because it taught me to have a sense of humor, laugh at myself, and to never let myself choose to be offended over meaningless issues. I thank God for all of it because all of it made me who I am today.

Let the word of Christ richly dwell within you, with all wisdom teaching and admonishing one another with psalms and hymns and spiritual songs, singing with thankfulness in your hearts to God. Colossians 3:15

As a mother, I look at my children and I understand more and more why my mother, despite knowing the joy and the blessing my accident brought me, can never rejoice over that incident. She carries the guilt of it and the weight of it, and no one can take that away or convince her it's not her fault. That's what we do as mothers.

Every day I try to make life easy for my own kids and to help them avoid pitfalls and situations that might hurt them. If they are hurt because I neglected to protect them, I swallow that guilt and live with it. Every time I try to protect them from the things in this world that might hurt them, I am reminded of the blessing my pain has been in my life. I am reminded of how intimate of a relationship I have with the Father because of the painful events I have experienced in my life.

I don't want to prevent my own children from growing through painful experiences, but I don't want them to hurt or suffer either.

My personal opinion is this is one of the scariest times to be a mother. It's not scary because there is so much danger out there. I was listening to someone not too long ago talk about how we live in the safest time in history, with the least amount of disease, death, and danger in recorded history. This is literally the safest the human race has ever been in history right now.

However, mothers are more scared now than ever before. We can't take our kids out of the house if someone sneezes for fear of illness. We can't even leave the house without a million contraptions, ointments, sunscreens, sprays, first aid kits, and survival kits for their safety. We are obsessed with safety, and the primary marketing technique for safety products is fear.

My mother sent me to spend the night with my friend when she had chicken pox so I would come down with chicken pox too, but now mothers are told it is deadly.

I remember my mother slapping her arm across my face in the car. That was my seat-belt growing up, but now babies are strapped in tighter than a NASCAR driver and ten year-olds are still in booster seats for safety reasons. In contrast, we had lawn chairs in the back of our van growing up.

We are told that old equipment is dangerous equipment, even though it worked fine for kids just three years earlier. Mothers are taught to be afraid of everything from the second the pregnancy test shows two lines.

I talked to a mother just the other day whose daughter is the same age as myself, and she said she had two pre-natal visits during her pregnancy four decades ago. TWO! Now we have dozens of visits and tests and interventions to prevent anything bad from happening. Everything about motherhood is scary because we are told it is scary, even though there has literally never been a safer time in history to have children.

In the midst of all the paranoia, our kids are growing up in a white washed, sanitized, padded life, preventing sneezes and boo-boos, missing out on what a fear-free life has to offer over a fear-full life. While the skinned knee hurts like fire, in that injury is the opportunity for Mama to hold her, kiss her boo-boo, and offer up an ice cream and bandage to make her feel better. When illness comes, so comes the opportunity to curl up on the couch and cuddle with mama while they watch their favorite cartoons and eat chicken noodle soup. The trials bring opportunity for us to slow down and love on each other. The trials give us opportunity to learn and grow. Just like our immune system is strengthened when exposed to various illness, our mind, body, and spirit are strengthened through trials.

The Bible tells us not to fear hundreds of times, and yet as mothers, fear is our number one motivator for everything we do with our kids, and ultimately, there is not one worry or action we can take to always, 100% of the time, protect our kids. Instead of fear, place those babies in the hands of the Almighty, surrendering them to the only One who can protect them 100% of the time, just as Hannah did with Samuel. When they suffer and experience pain, pray for them and realize the pain they feel may ultimately be the catalyst they need to go deeper with Jesus and to experience God in a new way. That pain may be the seed planted to make something beautiful grow. In fact, pain may be the obstacle they need to face in order to find salvation in Jesus Christ.

Don't hold them back in life worrying about what could happen, but trust God to care for them even when the "what might happen" happens. Be diligent to do your part and protect your kids, but don't let the fear of what could happen run your life and your kids' lives. Protect them, place them in God's hands, and then sit back and watch your kid and his life radiate the glory of Jesus Christ for the world to see.

The LORD is my light and my salvation;
Whom shall I fear?
The LORD is the defense of my life;
Whom shall I dread? Psalm 27:1

Contributors

TODAY, I WAS talking with a friend about homeschooling, and I began to quote the cliché statement about raising kids to be contributors to society. As I began the sentence, I realized that's not at all what I hope and wish for my kids. Not that I want them to be bums in society, but society is not my main concern nor was it ever my goal for homeschooling.

As I spoke, I changed my words as they fell out of my mouth to, "contributors to…

the Kingdom." Yes, we are first and foremost concerned with seeking and contributing to the Kingdom of God.

But seek first the kingdom of God and his righteousness, and all these things will be added to you. Matthew 6:33.

While I want my kids to learn to work and be kind and help others, I want them to learn to "Seek first the Kingdom of God."

I embraced homeschooling for the opportunity to teach my kids God's Word, His plan, His purpose for us, and His vision for their life.

Yet, somewhere along the way I have become bogged down in the acceptable outcomes of Western Civilization when it comes to raising my kids: good grades, friends, high test scores, awards, excellence in sports or extracurricular activities, scholarships, degrees, high paying and prestigious jobs, ...etc.

Honestly, I don't care if my kids accomplish any of it. If my children have everything every parent hopes for in their kid, but they don't know Jesus, I have failed them. If they know nothing of God's Word or their purpose on this earth to glorify Him in all they do, I have completely failed.

My hope and prayer is as I homeschool my kids and teach them to diagram sentences, multiply numbers, balance equations, and form a complete sentence, I will never forget my original goal and my ultimate plan to point them to Jesus and make them Kingdom builders.

I love the song by Need to Breathe, "Difference Maker". It says,

We are all transgressors, we're all sinners, we're all astronauts.
So if you're beating death then raise your hand but shut up if you're not
'Cause I am the difference maker

In the end, I want my kids to raise their hand and say, I'm beating death through Jesus Christ and you can too! I am a difference maker.

Teach your kids to contribute to the Kingdom because nothing else matters and everything else will fall into place when they do.

"Seek first the kingdom of God and His righteousness, and all these things will be added to you." Matthew 6:33

Have you ever thought about what "these things" might be? Jesus just spent the previous verses telling His people to stop worrying and to stop being afraid of the future. Just stop! God is sufficient. He will provide all your needs and care for you and your children better than you ever imagined, if you seek Him first.

Don't worry Mamas. Don't compare your kids to Norbert down the street while he finishes up his doctorate at five years-old. Don't buy into the fear your kids aren't learning the right things or understanding everything or making the grades like other homeschool kids. Don't let the pursuit of a superior education take over your joy and steal the message of Jesus Christ from them. Don't emphasize academics, forgetting the Kingdom is really what matters in this life. Teach them, Jesus first, and let the rest fall into place while you watch them live out a life as a Kingdom Builder.

You shall love the LORD *your God with all your heart and with all your soul and with all your might. "These words, which I am commanding you today, shall be on your heart.*

"You shall teach them diligently to your sons and shall talk of them when you sit in your house and when you walk by the way and when you lie down and when you rise up. "You shall bind them as a sign on your hand and they shall be as] frontals on your forehead. "You shall write them on the doorposts of your house and on your gates.

Deuteronomy 6:5-9

Surrender

YOUNG PEOPLE LEARN life, liberty and the pursuit of happiness is a fundamental, God-given right. It is a belief that makes our nation unique and a blessing in which to live. However, God never promises us liberty or happiness in the Christian life, and the majority of His children never experience the opportunity to pursue the American Dream of freedom, the benefits of an equal opportunity society and a quiet life.

My husband and I have been discussing at length the true meaning of becoming a believer and how it fits our understanding of God-given rights. The popular topic among adults says that the next generation feels entitled to just about anything without working for it, but God never says we are entitled to an easy, comfortable, American Dream type of life.

First, the Christian life is one of surrender. Jesus tells us to take up our cross and follow Him.

Then Jesus told his disciples, "If anyone would come after me, let him deny himself and take up his cross and follow me. Matthew 16:24

We hear it so much that it becomes so meaningless, especially as Americans. In comparison to the rest of the world, we are rich. Even some of the poorest of the USA are rich in comparison to the majority of this world.

I say to my kids all the time, "we don't have the money," but the truth is, while I may not have the money for a brand new $60,000 car, I am still far more endowed with an old clunker to drive than many mothers in this world. Some mothers have their own two feet and not much else. Every morning I wake up and turn on the hot shower first thing in the morning, while around the world other mothers wake up and walk miles to gather a pot of water for cooking, never considering they could have a hot shower during the day.

I fawn over clothing, the latest trendy shoes, or cutesy T-shirt with a Christian saying on it like, *I love Jesus and Naps,* while some mothers wake up and wash their family's one change of clothing in the local river that is also used as a public toilet.

I just can't wrap my head around magnitude of the blessings I experience, and I would say, never, not even one day, am I truly required to "take up my cross" in the same way the early Christians or the persecuted Christians around the world surrender daily. My cross sits nicely in the corner of my living room, among all my Hobby Lobby decorations, for all to see, making a cute, rustic, and significant statement that "I'm a Christian" in a time and place that it is not difficult in the least, to be a Christian.

Opportunities abound all around me to sacrifice and step out of my comfortable lifestyle. Seeking the Kingdom means we live out the Kingdom, and that means we do the hard stuff, stay up late for youth groups, take our free time to prepare a lesson for children' church or simply take time to be a friend. It means we don't always spend our time doing what we love, but rather doing what God gives us because we love Him more. Without the willingness to put aside my own desires and comfort, I will never experience the working of the Holy Spirit in the way Paul and Peter and Barnabas did. I will never see the mighty works of God or those around me glorify Him because of what He works through me. While taking up my cross may not require my life, am I willing to lead my family into a place where it takes up my time, my money and my energy? It's worth it.

Family Illness

THE FLU HIT our house last week, and all members of the family dropped like flies, except me. Six people with the flu, and little old me trying to take care of all of them. Do you know about the man flu? That one was the worst!

It's been almost a full two weeks and they still lay around all day with a few still coughing. Finally, last night was the first night I was able to sleep the whole night through without a coughing alarm every thirty minutes. My body has now adapted to the night time needs of the flu ridden, so despite the lack of coughing coming from the other bedrooms, I still woke up about every thirty minutes. My husband yelling out in his sleep didn't help any either.

It happens even to the most diligent, crunchy, healthy-minded Mama. Illness comes despite even the best efforts to ward it off. When it comes, it takes the entire family to the woodshed, and Mama usually emerges beaten and bruised the most.

Typically, I am the worst of all the sickly ones. My immune system is by far the weakest in the family, and I recently had surgery making it even weaker. However, I have no doubt that the Lord Jesus Christ was watching over our family this week, because if I had the flu, I never even knew it. In fact, I felt better mentally and physically than I have in months, with an abundant amount of energy, and the uncanny ability to cheerfully climb out of bed every hour and take care of sick kids. I was strengthened, and I don't believe it was because of any vitamin I took. Jesus strengthened me, plain and simple.

Each member of the family took ill one day after another, adding a new sick person every day, until day six, Easter Sunday, all six members of my family had fallen ill. This made the situation far worse considering my husband is a pastor. He preached, and then he crashed. Easter Sunday at our church did not go quite as we had planned because of our handicap in the week leading up to it, but he made it through anyway. I stayed home with all the other sick ones, serving, cleaning, and cooking. I drew special baths, made special juice, refilled the diffusers and humidifiers, applied special balms, washed clothes and blankets, found movie after movie on the internet, and sprayed my house down continually with sanitizer.

Through it all I never felt tired or overworked or discouraged. I hated watching my family feel so bad, but at the same time I relished the time to do what I do

> *I am the most important person when they all feel bad.*

best. At this point in their lives, I am the most important person when they feel this bad. They want no one but me. When I wasn't taking care of business, I held hot, sweaty kids that coughed and sneezed in my face, and I loved every minute of the privilege to be Mama. They needed someone, and I was that someone. I am the one living human being on this entire planet that can comfort their discomfort.

The pinnacle came when my youngest struggled to breath. He has a condition that is similar to asthma, causing major respiratory issues when he has a virus that causes swelling in his bronchial.

He began to labor in his breathing to the point that I had my panic button ready to activate for the ER. In my Mommy wisdom, I took him to the bathroom filled with steam and sat him on the side of the tub. Minutes passed, and his chest began to expand instead of sink, his shoulders dropped as he relaxed and stared at the floor finally taking some air into his lungs. He could barely speak, and his body showed its exhaustion at the battle it had been fighting for air. Despite his exhaustion, without raising his head, he pushed out of his little body, in his little baby voice a weak but heartfelt, "Thank you."

My heart melted. I just did what mothers do, that is take care of their babies. I never expect a "thank you" for helping them do something as basic as breathe, but in that moment I understood how much I meant to him as his mother. I am not just the arms that held him while his body ached, or made him refreshing juice to quench his dry mouth, or provided a mental escape from the discomfort he felt, **but I am also his lifeline**. When he faces his greatest crises, in my Mommy wisdom I guide him to a place of calm and peace while he battles that monster. I guide him to the place where there is relief and wait with him until relief comes, right by his side, holding him and singing and talking to him the entire time.

Only parents experience a relationship which mimics the Father we have in heaven during our times of crises. He calms our body, mind, heart, and spirit in the midst of a life threatening crises. In His divine wisdom, He guides us to the place of healing, and holds us while we wait for the healing to come, and when in our weakness we say, "Thank you", He melts at our expression of love for Him.

As much as I love to be their hero and their place of comfort, God wants the same from us. He wants us to run to him when we can't breathe and seek His arms of comfort, His wisdom for solutions, and his Words of peace.

Psalm 139:1-16 comes to mind when I think of this last bout with illness. David wrote it as a worship song *to* God, but I imagine God speaking to *me* as a child in his lap, like a lullaby, the way I speak to my children in the midst of their crisis.

I, the Lord, I have searched you and I know you!
I know when you sit down and when you rise up. I discern your thoughts from afar.
I search out your path and your lying down and I am acquainted with all your ways.
Even before a word was on your tongue, behold, I the Lord, I know it altogether.
I hem you in, behind and before, and lay my hand upon you.
Such knowledge is too wonderful for you; it is high; you cannot attain it.
Where shall you go from my Spirit? Or where shall you flee from my presence?

*If you ascend to heaven, I am there! If you make your bed
in Sheol, I am there!*

*If you take the wings of the morning and dwell in the
uttermost parts of the sea, even there my hand shall lead
you, and my right hand shall hold you.*

*If you say, "Surely the darkness covers me, and the light
about me be night," even the darkness is not dark to me;
the night is bright as the day, for darkness is as light with
me.*

*For I formed your inward part; I knitted you together in
your mother's womb.*

Praise me, for you are fearfully and wonderfully made.

Wonderful are my works; your soul knows it very well.

*Your frame was not hidden from me, when you were being
made in secret, intricately woven in the depths of the earth.*

*My eyes saw your unformed substance; in my book were
written, every one of them, the days that were formed for
you, when as yet there was none of them.*

The rest of Psalm 139 is the perfect "Thank you".

*How precious to me are your thoughts, O God! How vast is the
sum of them! If I would count them, they are more than the sand.
I awake and I am still with you. Psalm 139:17-18*

*Search me O God, and know my heart! Try me and know my
thoughts! And see if there be any grievous way in me, and lead me
in the way everlasting! Psalm 139:23-24*

Contentment

I WOULD SAY without a doubt; my greatest struggle is contentment. It blows me away that while I have more possessions and comfort than ninety percent of the world's population, I still find myself discontent.

Happiness, as the world defines happiness, is not a promise God ever gives to His people in the Bible.

Hey Noah, build a boat for 100 years while all the people around you ridicule and mock you and shun you. When you finish that task, I'll send every animal on earth to live on the boat with you and you can take care of them

I'm not sure I would've signed on the dotted line for that task

while it rains for forty days. After a year on the boat with no one but your wife, sons, and daughters-in-law, you can get off the boat, but there won't be any trees or vegetation. The flood will destroy all of it, so the only shelter you will have for decades will be this boat or a cave. Oh, and all the people will be gone except your family. I'm not sure I would've signed on the dotted line for that task.

Hey Joseph, I'm going to give you these dreams which will make your brothers hate you and sell you into slavery. Don't worry, you won't be a slave long. Eventually you'll go to prison. After a short twenty years though, you'll reign as second in command of the most powerful nation, and I'll bring those brothers back into your life so you can forgive them and save their lives, like the dreams I gave you in the first place promised they would.

Again, doesn't sound like my kind of plan for my life, especially as the favored, miracle, child.

Hey Jeremiah, I want you to serve under the next five kings telling Judah to repent, but they won't listen to you. In fact, they will beat you and imprison you and fight against you the entire time, and eventually they will be enslaved or destroyed anyway, and you'll have to watch all your people die a horrible death at the hands of your enemies.

Nope. No thanks I'm out.

Again and again, God called His people out to accomplish His plan and His will, but it never included the promise of happiness. It required obedience, and the reward was God himself which is far greater than happiness.

This life called motherhood is much the same. If we told expecting mothers what was truly in store for them, many might change their minds. The same is true of mothers on the brink of homeschooling; if they only knew what lay in store for them and all the days that end with the crushing feelings of failure, exhaustion, and hopelessness, buried under a house full of dirt, books, science experiments and half-eaten peanut butter and jelly sandwiches with a side of cold coffee.

While the decision to pick up our cross and surrender may bring heartache, illness, struggles, rejection, beatings, or failure, the end result is better than the American Dream of wealth and happiness. It's a joy-filled life and the wealth of heaven, an eternity spent with Jesus Christ.

The same holds true for motherhood and homeschooling. The reward for enduring the pain and agony, late nights and endless questions, is not just happiness. It's better than having a straight-A kid that becomes a successful adult in his field. It's the reward of raising them in the knowledge of Jesus Christ. It is being obedient to the point of studying algebraic equations in order to train these little Christ-followers, and in obedience, being rewarded by your Heavenly Father when they go to college and have a firm foundation that saves them from the pitfalls of sin.

Who knows what that "Mom Crown" in Heaven will look like. I suspect it will be made from construction paper with hand prints around the crown and stick on jewels because we all know that no precious stone is as precious as those little one's hand prints, love notes, and "I love you Mom" creations. The crowns that we earn because of the stewardship of our children as the Kingdom is concerned will be the most precious at Jesus' feet, no matter how modest. Because next to praying for them, the training of our children to love Jesus, obey His word, and walk with Him throughout their life, is the most urgent task we have as a mother. Grades, sports, awards, and accomplishments are all meaningless if they don't have a firm foundation in Jesus Christ.

It is our job, to teach our kids that the pursuit of holiness, righteousness, goodness, godliness, and most of all, obedience, is the command of the Bible. Pursuing happiness out of disobedience, results in death. Teach them to choose the greater.

For whoever would save his life will lose it, but whoever loses his life for my sake will find it.

For what will it profit a man if he gains the whole world and forfeits his soul? Or what shall a man give in return for his soul? Matthew 16:25-26

Fear Not

TODAY IS A tough day for our nation. Something horrific happened. A man decided, for some unknown reason as of yet, that ending the lives of dozens of people and injuring even more would satisfy whatever it was inside him that was hurting.

Upon waking and finding the news everywhere, my chest tightened and my eyes swelled with tears. Last Monday I woke to hear about another man that did the same thing in a church, killing the pastor and some church members.

Fear threatens to take over as a pastor's wife. Fear comes roaring into my heart wondering if my children will ever be safe in a large crowd or major event. Moreover, I wonder what the world will look like when they have children.

Most of all, fear threatens my happy little home life. Do I tell my children what has happened this week and fill them in on the evil that prowls around this earth, seeking whom he may devour? Or do I let them continue to live in blissful ignorance, at least for now? They will soon be introduced to all the world has to offer, so why not let them enjoy their innocence a little longer?

The day is almost over, and I still don't have the answer. I still haven't told my kids, and since we don't have cable or television, they won't know, at least not for a little while longer.

I wish I could say tomorrow it will mostly be forgotten, and I won't ever worry or fear again as to what dangers lie in wait in this world, but that just simply isn't true. The ruler of this world is evil, and his end goal is to destroy the human race. Christians and missionaries die every day for their faith. Children and adults alike are enslaved in numbers never known before, to be used up like toilet paper for another person's pleasure. People will steal, kill and destroy each other because evil is alive and well.

Illness will grip someone today and end another, sending them to their eternal resting place. It's here, and it's not going away. It feels endless and hopeless, and the only answer I have to give my kids, to give them the strength to live in such a place, is to tell them Jesus won victory over our sin and our death the day he rose from the dead. There is nothing this world can do to us if we are in Jesus. Praise God we have freedom from fear in Jesus!

Though a host encamp against me, My heart will not fear, though war rise against me, In spite of this I shall be confident Psalms 27:3

"In Christ Alone"
Stuart Townend and Keith Getty

No guilt in life, no fear in death,
This is the power of Christ in me,
From life's first cry, til final breath
Jesus commands my destiny
No power of hell, nor scheme
                of man
Can ever pluck me from His hand
Til He returns, or calls me home,

Here in the power of Christ I stand.

On Valentine's Day

ONE OF MY favorite family traditions stems from Valentine's Day. I will never forget the Valentine's Day when I received a heart necklace from my dad in the mail. That moment I opened the gift and saw my father had sent me a special Valentine's Day gift, I felt loved and desired, even more so than if it had come from a boy in my class. In fact, there was a boy that bought me Valentine's and birthday presents, yet it meant very little to me. A gift from my father, someone that I love, meant everything.

One day I want my children to experience the same sense of love and acceptance from their parents every Valentine's Day, especially as our world grows increasingly dependent on their relationship status for their self-worth. Instead of worrying about their relationship status with someone of the opposite sex, I've wanted my children to look forward to Valentine's Day as a day for their parents to express love for them as well as a day to remember all those believers that loved Jesus so much they gave their life for him, just as St. Valentine did so long ago.

Our tradition consists of a special Valentine's meal with a small gift to the boys from mom and a small gift to the girl from Dad. It's a gift of chocolate and the message, "I love you."

This year I tried something new based on a fellow mom's suggestion and wrote encouraging notes on hearts for my kids. I posted one on their door every night through the week leading up to Valentine's Day and included messages as simple as, "I love you", to "You are a great guitar player", to "I love how kind and considerate you are."

I learned an important lesson while I wrote these messages and thought about appropriate personal love notes for each of my five children. I learned they are indeed special, unique, and a great blessing to me. Taking the time to write them love notes changed my heart, making it easier in the following days. I learned that just as I need to take the time to be grateful to God for all He has done, to keep my focus on my blessings rather than my hardships, I need to focus on my children's attributes more than their faults.

I struggle to remember the greatest part of my job as a parent is encouraging and cheering them on because I tend to focus on the correction side of it. While much of parenting is correction, it is also loving and encouraging them too, with affirmations. When I take the time to meditate on the positive aspects of my children, I enjoy them more, take more time to appreciate their individuality and gifts they bring to our family, and become slower to blow my top in anger when they mess up. Anything that makes my day go smoother and makes my kids feel loved is a win in my book. Now I will make more of an effort and look for even more opportunities to speak or write encouraging words of life to my children.

Death and life are in the power of the tongue, and those who love it will eat its fruits. Proverbs 18:21

Winter Blues

IT'S FEBRUARY, AND this is the time of year I begin to wonder if I am going to survive yet another year of school. I have four whole months left of school, and school is just the beginning of my stress. Spring is filled with one birthday after another, our extracurricular activities start to take off in full swing, and little holidays abound. I'm not a Pinterest mom, but I do try to make some days special for my kids and my husband. My goal has always been to build good memories for my kids so that they can remember our time together as a family with fondness.

However, right in the depth of winter, when I am desperate for some sunlight on my face and a nice warm walk to move some of cold, stagnant blood of mine, I feel absolutely down in the dumps.

My emotions take a roller coaster ride as my stress and desperation go up, and my heart begins to believe the lies my mind keeps speaking.

- I have nothing to look forward to.
- My life is just a monotony of handing out commands, teaching subjects I loathe, and mountains of laundry.
- There will be no fun for us for weeks and weeks.
- I'm stuck at home, with all the work, while he gets to go out and do all kinds of fun things.

• Dad's the fun one and I am the dreaded teacher and disciplinarian.

The lies continue on and on after they sneak up on me, ambushing my happy little days with my kids. Some people love winter. For me the grey skies and frigid temperatures make me depressed.

On top of all the busyness, the drabness, and the seemingly endless chores, I become keenly aware of what we have not accomplished for the year. Maybe I took a week off from science before Christmas, and I have yet to pick it up again. Now my kids' education is neglected too because I am a failure as a homeschool mother. The papers needing a grade are piling up, and I have no idea if my children have mastered the last 4 chapters of their math because I lack the motivation to grade.

My life becomes a multitude of emotions from depression, to guilt, to burdensome feelings of overwhelming responsibility, to hopelessness. Rarely do I find a moment of joy and choose to dwell there.

That's the key. I reach the pinnacle of unhappiness and realize, this isn't where I want to live, so where's the exit to this place.

For me, my exit is first, some fun without kids and then some fun with my kids. My brain and my heart are reset when I take time to have fun as a human being and not mom. Fun mom is the one *providing* fun, not *having* fun. Taking my kids out for a day of fun before taking some fun time for myself first, will only add to my current state of depression. I need time to be just plain old Amy without any little human responsibilities.

Mom mode never completely shuts down after the first baby arrives, but it can be put on autopilot for a while. There are supermoms out there who would make others feel bad for needing time away from their kids, the ones that seem to love every single moment and aspect of being a mother. I admittedly do not love every single moment. I hate the moments when my kid lies to me and the moments when I'm cleaning up throw-up. I hate the moments when all five of them are asking me questions at the same time, and I can't make a decision for even one of them. I hate the moments when they are sick and suffering, or the moments when they've had a scary nightmare, and I'm hugging their shivering body to try to calm their spirit. I hate the moments when another kids hurts their feelings, and I hate the moments they hurt another kid's feelings even more. I hate watching them struggle with sin, and I hate the moments I lose all self-control and treat them in an undeserved way.

Parenting is messy and ugly and not at all attractive and enjoyable every second of the day. On the other hand, there are plenty of days it is the most rewarding of all, but in order to see through the muck and mess, I need time to recharge and reset away from those little gifts from God.

Don't feel guilty for needing time away from your charges. Jesus needed time. He frequently went away from his disciples, *His* charges, to be alone, to pray, and recharge. In fact, He even went away to simply sleep when they were on the boat and the storm came up. Jesus left his men and went to sleep, guilt free. When the storm arrived and they panicked, Jesus was so guilt free He seemed to be a little annoyed they woke him up to inform him they believed they were going to die.

I wonder sometimes if Jesus calmed the storm and looked at the disciples and said, "There. You happy? I'm going back to sleep and the next person that wakes me up is going to be tossed in the sea! I mean it! I don't care if there's a storm, or the boats on fire, let me sleep! We have a lot to do tomorrow."

Every time Jesus took time away from his disciples to pray and recharge, something powerful happened immediately following. Even Jesus needed a respite to be prepared for the work God had planned for Him. God gave us the example in His creation we need a full day of rest once a week, and Jesus carried the example on throughout His ministry. He never pushed himself to the point of utter exhaustion.

When the February blues begin to take me down, I remember even our Lord Jesus Christ followed the command to rest, and I am no stronger than He.

Rest

"This is rest; give rest to the weary; and this is repose; yet they would not hear." Isaiah 28:12

Isaiah warned Israel to find their rest in God, but they refused. Isaiah tells us in verse 13 the result of not resting in God.

that they may go, and fall backward, and be broken, and snared, and taken. Isaiah 28:13

I resist rest because I am afraid it will make others see me as weak or lazy. Even more I am afraid that if I take the time to rest, it will prove my greatest fear: I am unable to be a good mother.

The truth is, I *am* unable to be a good mother apart from Jesus, and if I am abiding in Him, I take the time to rest. Taking time to rest, like He commanded, and following His example is how I practice obedience. That is what I must do to be a good mother. Otherwise I am going to fall backward and be broken.

The same is true of marriage. Parents need time away from their kids so their marriage doesn't break in two. Go find some rest Mama. It's worth it, and your husband and kids are worth it.

Wherever You Are

CONTENTMENT IS ONE of my greatest struggles. All my life I've dealt with three issues in my heart; worry, fear, and contentment.

I never realized how discontent I allowed myself to be until I reached adulthood. I always felt grateful for what I had and how I lived however, that tiny parasite of discontent would weasel its way into my heart and mind and wreak havoc on all those blessings.

I didn't understand until God held me down through many uncomfortable situations, stripping me of my pride in my own efforts and my ability to soothe my own discomfort all while providing me with everything I need and nothing that I want.

It was in those times I was forced to really embrace the idea Jim Elliot spoke, "Where ever you are, be all there."

The feel-good quotes that roam around out there in our world say things like, "Follow your heart," "Chase your dreams," "If you don't like your life, change it," and so on. However, what do you do when you literally are held back by the Almighty from chasing your dreams and changing your life?

The truth is our heart's desire should be to follow the heart of God, not our own sinful, deceitful heart.

"The heart is deceitful above all things and beyond cure," Jeremiah 17:9

Our dreams should be the same as our Father's, and what does He desire more than anything? Us. He desires none should perish. His dream is to see the people of the world evangelized with the Gospel. What other dream is worth pursuing?

If you don't like your life, change it.

"The heart of man plans his way, but the LORD establishes his steps." Proverbs 16:9

If you don't like your life, it's not your life that needs to change, it's your focus and your attitude.

106

"But Seek first the Kingdom of God and His righteousness, and all these things will be added to you." Matthew 6:33

When we seek after God and ask Him to give us exactly what we need right now, we can stop chasing success. We will never be content with success we achieve on our own. If we trust in Jesus, He will, every time, bring us to the exact place we should be to accomplish His plan this day, and the only place that will bring true contentment. This is what Jim Elliot meant. The day you spend hours at the DMV, He has a plan for you to be there. Most often we are too busy being discontent and complaining to recognize the task He has for us right where we are. One of my favorite verses, especially for my children is;

"Do all things without grumbling or disputing, so that you may be blameless and innocent, children of God without blemish in the midst of a crooked and twisted generation, among whom you shine as lights in this world."
Phil. 2:14-15

An attitude of discontent extinguishes the light He put inside us. The complaining and grumbling overshadows His light. I know now my discomfort was forced upon me to force the grumbling out of my heart so that my light could shine.

Discontentment stole my love and kindness, and without love, I lost the ability to be obedient to my calling. Every time I felt my chest tighten in frustration toward my situation, I prayed that God would turn that discomfort and discontent, to contentment and gratitude. He answered every single time.

I was telling Jay one day how I prayed and prayed God would change him so we could move on from one situation or another, and God came through. God changed his heart and or our situation every time. Jay chuckled and confessed, I have prayed many times for God to change you, but I never once considered you were praying for me.

When you find yourself unhappy and discontent, whether it is in your school, your home, your church, your community, your job, and especially your marriage, ask God if the matter is a situational issue that needs to change and if there is action you need to take to change the situation, or is it simply a matter of the condition of your heart? Does your attitude instead of your situation need to change? Ask him to give you a change of heart or situation. He will answer every time!

Learning

ONE OF MY greatest joys in life is when my children are excited about what they have learned for the day. My 14 year-old is studying the Constitution and every day he comes out of his room and says, "Guess what I learned today!"

While he recounts the day's lessons and the discovery of the amazing gift of our Constitution, I find solace in my efforts in their education. While I might feel like a failure in so many ways, his excitement gives me hope they will grow into adults with some knowledge, but even more, they will grow into adults who want to learn, know how to learn, and continually educate themselves.

I knew from the beginning I wanted my children to be able to learn independently, not just ingest and regurgitate facts, but truly learn, and learn how to learn. I saw myself as the guide on a journey, giving them the tools they need to ingest the knowledge they need, not force feeding it to them.

I quickly learned with my oldest that simply putting a book out in plain sight, whether it is on the kitchen table or coffee table, will inevitably result in him picking it up and reading without any prompting. He is simply that kind of kid. I am jealous of his ability to read anything. While my reading material must be entertaining from the first sentence, he can push through and read the most boring of books and gain the knowledge it contains.

My second child must be convinced he needs to read something. I must push and prod him, but once he has been given his daily dose of knowledge, he becomes excited about what he learned for the day.

My third kid becomes easily overwhelmed. He is an excellent reader and retains the knowledge, but when I say, "Read four chapters today," it is daunting to him. I either break his work up into bite sized pieces for him, or I encourage him in his ability. He always comes through despite his own self-doubt.

My fourth kid is in her own little world, but delights in anything girly. It's not a surprise considering she's the only girl with four brothers. She wants all the girl things. She wants all the good things. Most of all, she wants the approval and validation of her parents, therefore she will read, just for the outcome of praise. However, she loves to gain new knowledge as well.

My baby is just six years-old and he is learning to read. He fights me. He declares he can't read despite the fact he was the easiest of all five to teach to read. He shows his frustration quite often declaring that reading is impossible, yet he can read better than most middle school kids. Usually I handle his fits and his frustrations by agreeing. "English is difficult. It makes no sense so often, but you are mastering it beautifully, Little One." He can pick up a book and read it, and it even surprises him when he masters the words so easily.

Most of my days seem daunting and teaching five different grades all at once is a heavy burden and responsibility to carry. I tend to focus on my failures and my shortcomings as a mother and a teacher more than I celebrate our victories. Just recording my days through these short devotionals has revealed this truth to me.

It is time to celebrate! These kids may not meet my expectations or my plans for the year, but my goodness they are making strides and accomplishing far more than I ever did at their age. That is something to celebrate!

Accomplishments

A FOURTEEN YEAR-OLD excited about the Constitution is something to celebrate. A six year-old reading his Bible daily is a victory!

With this reflection, I wanted to reach out to the homeschool moms like myself, the ones that feel defeated more often than victorious. I wanted to speak to the moms that don't speak encouragement to themselves, but rather focus all their attention on all their own failures and flaws. Mostly I wanted to say,

Dear Sister, you are not alone! We all struggle and beat ourselves up far more than we realize. The moms whose kids are in public school, the ones whose kids are grown, the pastor and his wife, the teacher, and every single parent out there that cares an iota about their kids, struggle with feelings of failure and inadequacy. You, are not, alone.

Today however, I want to pour into you encouragement in your victories. Today, take the time to recognize the accomplishments. Don't compare today to yesterday. Compare today to last year and take a mental note of how far you and your children have come. Forget you are sixteen weeks behind in history, ten weeks behind in science, and the box of supplies for art is still sitting there unopened. Forget that you spent more time nursing a sick baby than teaching the first grader to read while he is now almost finished with first grade and still learning his first words. Forget all those shortcomings and those benchmarks you set for yourself as a homeschool mom and celebrate your victories. If you can't find any, ask God to show you where they may be, because they are there. Do your kids go to bed feeling loved? Then you have victory in their heart. Did they laugh and smile today? That is a victory.

Most of all, take it from a mom with kids reaching the end of their homeschool career. While most of what you wanted to accomplish never happened, the end results are more than acceptable. If those kids learn to love God and His Word, if they know you love them, and if they are seeking to serve God in whatever capacity He calls them, then you're okay, Mama, and so are

they! Pat yourself on the back and have some cake for lunch, not just left over chicken nuggets. I can't help but sing, "Accentuate the positive, eliminate the negative..." That's Biblical you know.

"Finally [sisters], whatever is true, whatever is honorable, whatever is just, whatever is pure, whatever is lovely, whatever is commendable, if there is any excellence, if there is anything worthy of praise, think about these things. What you have learned and received and heard and see in in me-practice these things, and the God of peace will be with you." Philippians 4:8-10

Treasure

WHAT IS IMPORTANT to you? This one little question and a short little story has been turning over and over in my mind for days now.

I recently read a story about a former pastor that took an Uber from the airport. As they drove, the driver asked him, "What's important to you?"

It turned out the driver was a former pastor as well.

The story and the question struck me for so many reasons. First, as a stay-at-home mom, I rarely meet new people. Sharing the good news of Jesus with the lost must be intentional on my part because I rarely talk to people outside my family, church, library and grocery store.

I realized this was an excellent way to strike up a meaningful conversation with strangers when I do have the privilege to meet new people. I am excited to try it out one day soon and see where it leads.

Second, it made me question how I might answer that question. Even more, would my actions match up to my answer?

I would say the important places in my life are my family

Will my actions match my words?

and my faith. Jesus, husband, kids, church, and extended family. That's my list. However, I evaluated my behavior to find if those people were truly what I valued. Do I truly value Jesus above all else? Am I spending time with Him, going to Him with my good news and my bad news, my thanksgivings and my need for help? Am I walking with Him? Some days He is on my mind but definitely not my priority 100% of the time. Honestly, the majority of the time I make myself my first priority.

My husband is a little easier. I spend time with him every day. Half of what I do in a day is for him. However, some days I am bitter toward him or angry at him for not meeting my expectations, and I treat him as anything but important.

My kids are definitely important to me. My whole life revolves around their needs, but just like my husband, my behavior may say otherwise. Some mornings I wake up and pray, "Lord, help me to treat them like the precious treasures they are." Some mornings I wake up and say, "And so it begins." Some days I treat them more like burdens than blessings. More than that, my mouth rarely expresses to them the blessing they are in my life. Quite often I complain or whine about my lot in life as a mother, a privilege denied to many women. I tell my children to be a blessing and not a burden. However, some days I need to remember they *are* a blessing, even when they make me crazy with whining or questions or messes or quarrels or needs. It starts in the heart.

"Wherever your treasure is, there your heart will be also."
Matthew 6:21

If my mouth speaks ill of my children, and it flows from my heart, then it reveals that faith and family may not be my treasure after all. When my heart is filled with anger, bitterness, self-pity, selfishness, or simply worldly things instead of God's Word, it will flow into all the areas of my life, stealing the treasures God has granted.

Not one bad day makes for a filthy heart. There will be bad days, and bad moments, but those bad moments should not overshadow the good times and change the focus of our hearts from what we desire to be important to us.

After my last baby was born, I became so ill I could not get myself out of bed. At first, every doctor looked at my bloodwork and said, "You're fine, it must be psychological. Want some Prozac?" I knew my problem wasn't psychological, even though my illness manifested with mood swings and rage. I finally began a long list of ailments, starting with low thyroid, and ending with a fatty liver. Basically, my body didn't work, so it wasn't being fed, and the result was a very tired and sick Mama that just wanted to be able to enjoy her kids.

One day, my chiropractor told me, "So if you wake up and you don't feel good, that's okay. It's a bad day, but that doesn't mean the next day is going to be a bad day. You reset, you get through the day and look forward to the good day." That little talk changed my life. I suddenly realized I was living life as if I was already dead, rather than taking it one day at a time. Pretty soon, I realized I had more good days than bad, and when I bad day came, I didn't make it worse by wallowing, but rather rested looking forward to the next good day. Instead of whining to God about my condition, I began to pray for His strength in those bad days, and for the next good day to come quickly.

It's been almost seven years since I first found myself unable to live, and I am still working toward healthy and living with autoimmune disease and a broken body. I do it because those that are important to me are worth it, and because a life lived as a pity party does not glorify God, the most important One of all.

It always goes back to the simple Sunday School answers doesn't it. Jesus. That's who it's all about.

Touch

MOST OF MY children, not all, I have found learn so much better from my lap. When they sit apart from me, and we work on some new concept, they often end up frustrated, which in turn frustrates me. I discovered a long time ago that just placing my hand on my child's shoulder

The touch of a mother is truly full of power

or putting my arms around them during their time of learning, eases his or her frustrations, calms them down, and results in better scholastic performance. It amazes me my touch can do so much to their brain, their emotions, their well-being, and their physical state.

The touch of a mother is truly full of power. After my injury as a child, my mother always said she knew when I was in pain because she felt my pain; she had sympathy pains. I always thought that was weird until my son broke his clavicle. Anytime I touched his shoulder I felt physical pain throughout my body, until it was healed. I needed no x-ray to tell me it was healed because when it had healed, I no longer felt his pain. The world would say magical; I say divine. God gave mothers a unique, innate discernment when it comes to her children. After all, their DNA exists in her own body until the day she dies. They literally become part of her.

It was in this realization when I took my 5th child into my lap, just as I had done with his four older siblings as they learned to read, that he relaxed, and I realized the power and responsibility I have over my children. My nine-year-old, as she is learning, still sits as close to me as she possibly can, while she rubs my arm with her hand, something she started as an infant while I nursed her. My teenagers no longer snuggle up to me, but in the moments they are frustrated or angry at their school work or life, they never turn down a warm hug from their mother. In fact, my older boys, both of which are much taller than me, lean in and find comfort in my embrace still, although they both could hold me like a child.

God compares Himself to a mother, possessing the same qualities as a mother many times throughout the Bible. He protects like a mama bear (Hosea 13:8), He loves and provides sustenance (Hosea 11:3-4), covers and protects like a mother eagle (Deuteronomy 32:18), and comforts (Isaiah 66:13).

If my touch as a mother is so powerful I can calm and comfort, imagine how much more God's touch can change our lives. Holding my injured, angry, frustrated, sad, hurt, or upset child can bring instant peace into their lives. Likewise, running to the lap of our Heavenly Father can bring the peace we need in our times of need. So often I run to anything but the only One who can truly heal me, finally caving to the idea "I guess all I can do is just pray." Just pray? All? Prayer is everything!

Like a child runs to his mother, run to the Father and ask for strength, healing, comfort, protection, and sustenance, whatever the need may be. He will hold you snug and secure you in His lap, giving you everything you need. When you call for help, He is already there.

Sacrifice

ONE OF THE most difficult aspects of homeschooling, almost every homeschool family shares, is sacrifice. The sacrifices we make to be able to homeschool our children can wear a mom and dad down to the nub of their soul.

Most of us live on one income, or one income plus a supplemental, work at home, income that provides just a little extra.

While the world around us buys the expensive tennis shoes and electronics for their kids, we buy them science and math books. We pay for co-ops, music and art lessons, sports and dance.

In our family, we joke our kids don't need expensive clothing except for Sunday clothes because the rest of the week they spend half the day in their pajamas and the other half in their play clothes. To my dismay, there are still times I personally struggle not to compare myself to those around us.

I want the best for my kids in every aspect, but in order to homeschool, sacrifices must be made and sometimes we struggle to make ends meet.

Today my car broke. We were hit

In order to homeschool, sacrifices must be made

three months ago by another driver. Last

month we finally had that damage fixed only to find out there was a plethora of other issues that needed immediate attention. To be clear, our vehicle is almost twenty years old and has 266,000 miles on it. It is going to need some upkeep, but the sacrifice we have made in order to homeschool is to drive an older car and maintain it over taking on the debt of a newer car, at least for now.

This past weekend my husband spent his entire Saturday working on the brakes, the bearings, the ball joint, and the tires. Today, he barely made it to his destination when the wheel broke.

Needless to say, these are the kinds of days we feel completely defeated. We prayed God would provide for the previous fixes, and while God provided in amazing ways, we woke up feeling as if our car problems were behind us, only to be faced with the same problem again.

It's in these difficult times, the hungry years, that it's important stay focused and ignore the enemy's attacks and temptation to compare ourselves to those around us. We are not defeated or even deprived. We may be tired and unable to see how this will end up, but I do know that not once in all our eighteen years of marriage, has God completely abandoned us and not provided what we need. I am confident He is faithful and He will again provide.

As the day draws to an end, I draw near to what the Word says to me in 2 Corinthians 4:8-10, although I may be pressed and afflicted, I am not defeated.

> *"We are afflicted in every way, but not crushed; perplexed, but not driven to despair; persecuted, but not forsaken; struck down, but not destroyed; always carrying in the body the death of Jesus, so that the life of Jesus may also be manifested in our bodies."*
>
> *2 Corinthians 4:8-10*

When I think about the man who wrote those words and all he endured, I feel silly allowing a stupid little mechanical failure to make me feel like I can place myself in the same category at all. Paul was imprisoned, beaten, stoned, persecuted, shipwrecked, snake bitten, did I mention beaten? Yet, he never allowed himself to be described as destroyed or defeated.

While my trouble may not be as severe as Paul's, the trouble of a broken car is real. Trouble of any sort is real and heavy to the person carrying the burden. Even in those small difficulties in life, those little inconveniences that give us frustrations, Paul gave us a perfect example to follow. While he sat in jail, Paul praised Jesus. He worshiped, he sang, he gave thanks. He turned his eyes from the storm to the one who calms the storm and rejoiced.

While I find myself in a prison of frustration of my own making, I pray I will find the same courage to turn my eyes to the One that calms my storms, and give Him praise.

As the pressures of this world press in on you, I pray you will embrace the victory Jesus gave you, and let His life and His love, even in those times when life strikes you down, be visible to everyone.

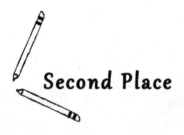

Second Place

WHEN MY HUSBAND was attending seminary in New Orleans and working, we didn't have enough to make ends meet. Through various emergencies, our savings dwindled down to almost nothing just ten months after we moved to New Orleans. I had a two year-old and a newborn, and I was starting to panic a little questioning from where our grocery money might come. It was the end of the pay period, and we had nothing. We were down to just a few groceries in our tiny apartment, and I was creating some interesting meals with what was in our cupboards.

The seminary held a spring family fest full of fun activities, one of which was a baking contest. Jay insisted I bake my banana bread with homemade caramel sauce and enter it into the contest. It just so happened I had all the ingredients to do so, despite our bare cupboards. "It's gonna win 1st place," he declared. "Nothing beats your banana bread."

I worked hard the night before, making sure it didn't just taste delicious, but that it looked delicious as well. It was a sight to behold, as all award winning confections should be.

The next day they announced the winners, and I won second place. I wasn't disappointed until I walked to the table to claim my prize. The first place winner was a single, young man that made a soupy, ugly tiramisu in a roaster pan! "That must taste amazing because it looks hideous!" I thought to myself. I stood back patiently as they handed him his prize, a three-ring binder with the seminary logo on the front. Next was my turn. The lady smiled and handed me a business letter size envelope. As I opened it, my eyes welled up with tears. It was the most beautiful love letter God could have sent me in the form of a gift certificate to the local grocery store. That night we had ice cream with the leftover banana bread, and we drank milk the next morning for breakfast. The certificate's value was just enough to get us through to the next pay period.

I don't know what was in that 3-ring binder the first place winner received, but I know without a doubt God knew even if my banana bread deserved first place, what I needed was second place. For the next two years, we watched as God provided every single morsel along the way.

I was constantly reminded of the Israelites and the gift of the manna they received. They were not given enough to last through the entire forty years of wandering, but rather for the day. Each day, God gave us just enough, and we learned some important lessons about contentment and pursing more than we needed.

While we could have pursued more, and probably even gained more in our pursuits, we might have missed the glory of God that came in the form of our daily manna. The true blessing wasn't in what we earned or what He provided, but in watching God provide every single day. Our hearts grew in ways they might never have grown otherwise. Our faith muscles strengthened. We learned to be grateful in every little blessing, and we excitedly waited for the solution to every single problem. It's been fourteen years since the day I won that gift certificate, and we still experience excitement waiting on God to provide for us. He never forgets, He's never late, and He always provides just enough.

A Beloved One

THIS LAST YEAR was a whirl wind for me. I feel as though it is the year I became an adult, at the tender age of thirty-nine. We moved 300 miles, started a new career, and moved into the ministry for which we've been preparing for almost twenty years. Our new home is everything we never knew we wanted. Jay is thriving in his ministry. Overall, we've experienced a wonderful year.

However, it was difficult as well. I lost two people I loved, my grandmother and my uncle.

First came my uncle's unexpected passing. Ricky was the type of person everyone loves. I learned just how much at his funeral. It was a packed room with people from all over the community that came to remember his life. He was gentle, mild and meek, amiable, witty, and so kind. He did not possess the typical characteristics of our family. We are loud, boisterous, mouthy, and prickly, but not Ricky.

The dark side of Ricky involved far too much alcohol. Drinking stole most of the good he found in his life. With each loss, whether it was in his career, his personal life  or his family, alcohol gained more control over him and his body. It turned to pancreatitis and eventually gall stones lodged in his liver and killed him. It only took a couple of days, and the little stone that could be removed through surgery wreaked so much havoc over his weak body it couldn't even survive the surgery. He died within 3 minutes of removing life support. My mother had asked him if he knew He would be going home to Jesus. He had blinked, assuring her he was okay.

After his death I wanted to know, what contribution did Ricky give to this world? What purpose was there for his more than sixty years of life? His entire adult life was tortured by alcohol, and he made no major accomplishments in work, family, or life. I needed to know this man I loved would be remembered for who he was and his kind heart and not what he did wrong.

Ricky and I were not close in that we sat and had long deep conversations. He didn't carry on long deep conversations with many people, but he did have an orneriness about him, giving my husband a good razzing every once in a while. My brother spent every day with him working on the farm and had a much closer relationship with him than I did from 300 miles away. He did, however, always make me feel loved and accepted for who I am. The rest of my family is brutally honest and has no problem offering their generous critique of my life choices, appearance, smell, situation, or whatever else they feel the need to "lovingly" correct, but not Ricky. Ricky just wanted to know if I was okay, happy, loved, and cared for. He never criticized me but always offered encouragement and praise, and he always had some cash to give me to help with travel expenses. Even at thirty-five years old I was still his little niece to whom he could slip a twenty-dollar bill. At one point, he even gave us a Suburban that became our family vehicle, free of any strings attached.

After his death, I walked through his home, dusty like a bachelor's house would be, and found that in his bedroom he had one picture: me. In this whole house, he kept one picture of me sitting on his dresser. At that point I had somewhat of an answer; Ricky loved me, and he was a great uncle. That alone gave his life meaning. The packed house at his funeral was more evidence that it wasn't just my life he impacted, but the community knew Ricky's love and kindness at some point as well.

Ricky may not have left a crater-sized mark on this earth, but he left a crater-sized mark on my life and everyone that had the privilege to know him. In the midst of my loud, critical family, after I was given those sometimes hurtful critiques, Ricky always lifted me up with his encouragement. He showed me that I can love someone without pointing out their flaws, or even noticing them. He taught me I can give to people, even in big ways, without expecting so much as a thank you. Ricky exemplified to me an ability to remain unresponsive and to stay quiet rather than quarrel over meaningless issues. Ricky taught me more than I realized.

As we left his funeral and headed home that sunny afternoon, my soul cried out in deep, painful sobs. I would never see him or feel his embrace again. His life was over, and I never even sent him a thank you card for my wedding present.

Every Father's Day I intended to send him a card just to say, "I love you and thank you for being my uncle." Every year I procrastinated until it was too late. Now I would never be able to send it. I know it's trite to say, tell the people you love them when you can because you never know when they'll be gone, but it is so true. Regret stinks.

It's been a year since his death, but I still think about him every day and work through the questions I have in my heart and mind about his life and his eternity. My prayer has been that while I have many reading and arithmetic lessons to teach my children, I teach them the most important lessons Ricky exemplified for me: a quiet and gentle spirit, encouragement void of criticism, unconditional love, kindness toward everyone, and genuine and selfless generosity. I pray nothing would gain such a hold on me it robs the world of the gifts God has given me, the way the alcohol robbed the world of the all the gifts God had given to Ricky. I pray even while it may not be drunkenness that prevents me from making the most of the time I have, I will never again let complacency, laziness, procrastination, busyness, or anything else that fights for my attention, waste my time, especially when it comes to the ones I love.

Most of all I pray that not one person I know will ever go to bed without knowing how much I love them, and above all, how much Jesus loves them.

Look carefully then how you walk, not as unwise but as wise, **making the best use of the time,** *because the days are evil. Therefore do not be foolish, but understand what the will of the Lord is, And do not get drunk with wine, for that is debauchery, but be filled with the Spirit, addressing one another in psalms and hymns and spiritual songs, singing and making melody to the Lord with your heart, giving thanks always and for everything to God the Father in the name of our Lord Jesus Christ, submitting to one another out of reverence for Christ. Ephesians 5:15-21*

Can I Have a
Do-Over Please?

LAST WEEKEND I took my three youngest children on a long road trip without my husband. This is a big deal because you see, I am an exceedingly spoiled wife. When we travel, I don't load the car, I don't take the bags up to the hotel room, I don't drive, I don't pump gas, and I don't take little boys to the bathroom. My husband relies on me to ensure the bags are packed properly, provide food and snacks, pleasant conversation, and a good night's sleep. That's my wheelhouse when traveling. He does the heavy lifting, and I make sure we're all happy and healthy.

However, this last weekend without him, I had to carry out his role as well as my own. Fortunately, my kids are old enough to be mostly independent, follow directions, and help with the burden, but the oldest of the three is only eleven and not quite old enough for me to feel comfortable relying on him for too much other than just assistance.

He is also my middle child. He is the middlest, middle child there ever was. He wants to be one of the big boys and do all they are allowed to do. He wanted to go to the youth group in the third grade and for the life of him, couldn't imagine why I wouldn't let him because, in his mind, he is just as old and mature as his older brothers. He wants nothing more than a phone for his twelfth birthday because his older brothers received a phone (just a simple flip phone with no internet) for their twelfth birthdays. That boy just wants to be grown-up, like yesterday.

At the same time, he wants all the pleasures and joys of being the little one too. He wants to go to the children's classes instead of the adult class the youth attend at church. He wants to be invited to all the birthday parties and eat cake too. He wants to be able to sleep with Mom and Dad when he's scared.

While my middle child is in many ways old enough to take some responsibility and help me when dad's not around, he is still a little one that needs to be watched over closely. He has not grown into a young man's body like my older teenagers, but he has an idea of what it means to be grown up.

At the end of this trip I was left with the Mama task of getting everyone packed again and ready to go, as well as taking all the luggage, pillows, stuffed animals, book bags, and acquired treasures down to the car from the ninth floor of the hotel. When we finally managed to wrangle the overloaded luggage cart down nine stories, through the lobby after checking out, and down another elevator to the parking garage, I made the comment to one of the hotel staff, "I don't usually have to do this. My husband does it for me, and I am really missing him now."

My middle boy that wants so desperately to be seen and regarded as a man, whined, "But you have me and I helped." My heart sank. He needed encouragement and validation as "the man" in charge on this trip. His dad had even told him, take care of your mom and brother and sister, and help her. I had not only disgraced him in that comment, but I had trampled all over his masculinity the entire morning. Every effort he made to help me, I had complained and griped and made it clear he wasn't doing anything right or helping me at all. The message I sent him said he is not a blessing to me, but rather a huge burden. While it was true that often times he created more work for me in his efforts to help, my attitude and my words dug in to insult and tear him down, rather than to teach and encourage.

At that moment, I realized, he needed to be a hero in my life, and I made him an annoying, burdensome toddler. Worst of all, there was nothing I could do to go back and change my attitude and my actions toward him. The damage was done.

As I began the long drive home, I recounted the weekend and all the times I discouraged him and made it clear he had messed up. I prayed, *God, is there any way I can get a do-over?*

I truly meant it, but I know I can't go back and change what happened. In my exhaustion and frustration, I was a jerk and not helpful to my son and his need for responsibility. I gave him no opportunity to be "the man" and help me. I stole from him the opportunity to learn lifelong lessons, and worst of all, an opportunity to build a deeper relationship with him. This had been a unique situation that rarely comes along. I had the opportunity to let him be the big brother. He is rarely the oldest in the crowd, but I blew it. Who knows when the opportunity will arise again. I prayed, "God, show me how to do better, and give me ideas to give him these opportunities in the future."

I decided from now on he can be the one that goes shopping for groceries with me, and in those times I can give him the opportunity to be strong and helpful. I can give him opportunities to be my hero, and the drive time can be a time we talk and connect.

Parenting pre-teens and teenagers is a game changer for me, because I was not a typical teenager. I was born grown up and responsible, never really facing the teenage years the same way as most teens, so I have no idea what to do with the typical teenage behaviors.

The focus of my parenting has changed from protection and correction to nurturing an adult mentality and letting go, especially with mothers and boys. Dr. James Dobson

> *The focus of parenting teen boys' changes to an adult mentality and letting go.*

talks about this phenomenon in his book *Bringing Up Boys*. He specifically says boys have to figuratively kill their mothers to declare their manhood. I have been dreading those years for over a decade, and while I have most certainly experienced some of that, my boys have always remained close to me. I even tease my fourteen year-old when he's pushing my limits, "I know you need to kill me to be a man, but can you please just lay off for a minute." He knows what I'm saying, and it usually diffuses the attitude and reconnects us as parent and child. I know he loves me and he doesn't want to hurt me, but that's my way of saying, "You are hurting me right now, so I will back off if you will too."

But this third one, throws me for a loop. We struggle more than the others because I can relate to him the least of all the kids. We don't butt heads,

On the brink of becoming a man, he needs to be someone's hero.

but we struggle to connect emotionally. He's always been the kid that doesn't want to be kissed by his mama, or hold her hand, or show he cares because that's embarrassing.

However, right now, as he is on the brink of becoming a young man, he needs to be a hero to someone, and more than anything I want him to be my hero. I want him to know that although our relationship struggled, I've always been his biggest fan.

Never miss the chance to give your kids opportunities to be responsible. They need your love, but they also need your trust and your respect. I realized with this kid, if I don't give him opportunities to be respected and trusted, he will stop trying. While kids need to learn obedience, parents must be careful to avoid exasperating their kids too. I pray for you today that your relationship with your kids, whatever their ages, is strong and full of mutual respect and trust. I pray you never miss a teaching opportunity and the opportunity to cheer your kid on to righteousness.

"Children obey your parents in everything, for this pleases the Lord. [Mothers] don't provoke your children, lest they become discouraged."
Colossians 3:20-21

WAKING UP

"For this very reason, make every effort to supplement your faith with virtue, and virtue with knowledge, and knowledge with self-control, and self-control with steadfastness, and steadfastness with godliness, and godliness with brotherly affection, and brotherly affection with love. For if these qualities are yours and are increasing they keep you from being ineffective or unfruitful in the knowledge of our Lord Jesus Christ. For whoever lacks these is so nearsighted that

he is blind, having forgotten that he was
cleansed from his former sins."
2 Peter 1:5-9

There was a movie not too long ago about a woman that went to bed every night and forgot everything, waking up in the morning not even knowing who she was. Her brain reset itself every morning. The woman left herself a video to watch every morning upon waking, to fill in the forgotten memory of who she was and why she remembered nothing.

Sometimes I feel like that woman. I forget who I am in an instant. I may go to bed full of the Holy Spirit and wake up completely empty.

Maybe it's a back ache, or a bad night's sleep, or the smoke alarm

You are the daughter of the King

going off at 6AM on my Saturday I have

the opportunity to sleep in because my son was cooking bacon before he and his father go hunting. Whatever the reason, I forget. I don't just forget who I am, I forget who God is. I've been thinking of how I might be able to leave myself a video to watch every morning.

You are the daughter of the King. Remember when He saved you from crashing into that semi-truck because you were distracted by your kids? Remember when you were so depressed you couldn't do anything but cry, but he healed your heart? God gave you the strength to make it through the day yesterday, when your daughter broke her collar bone so bad the bones were poking out of her shoulder. You were so exhausted, but He gave you the strength to take care of her.

Last week He gave you joy. It seemed like everything in the house was breaking and the bank account was empty. The final straw was the car. The alternator went out, but remember how you made dinner that night with a smile on your face, because you had an unexplainable joy?

Then there is your favorite story. You and your husband were struggling to make ends meet as he worked and attended seminary. You had burned through your savings to put food on the table, and your cupboards were empty for the next week, but you prayed and trusted that God would provide, and you received an unexpected check, just enough to buy some milk for the kids.

If only I could wake up every morning remembering from all that I have been saved. If only the first words off my lips were, "Good morning, Jesus," instead of "It's morning already?"

Fortunately, Peter tells us we don't need a video to remind us. He gives us the formula. I will be studying his list of virtues this week and sharing with you what God reveals.

Peter says to add to that faith virtue. Virtue means "moral excellence". Most of us have come at least that far first thing in the morning. Remain excellent in your morals. Do what's right and good.

Next Peter tells us to add to our virtue, knowledge. Start your day off with knowledge, a scripture, a study, anything from God's Word.

It seems easy enough. Become a believer in Jesus, straighten up your behavior, and dig into His word because all the rest will fall into place.

I still need to work on so many of my character flaws. Self-control being the first. Right now I sit here with an empty chocolate bar wrapper beside me. I intended to only eat one small piece. Oops.

Steadfastness. Isn't that the virtue homeschool moms need most? I don't know how many days I have decided I am too tired and too empty and too frustrated. These kids are going to public school. It's in those days I need steadfastness to be obedient to what God has called me. I need steadfastness to keep my head calm when kids lie or argue incessantly. I need a good dose of steadfastness, loyalty, devotions and dedication to this calling of motherhood and homeschooling.

Godliness seems easy enough. When I dig a little deep I ask, can I really say I have godliness in my pocket of virtues. Yes, on the outside I act as if I am Godly, but what about when I'm alone. Are my thoughts toward others, especially my husband and my kids, godly? Not always. I teach my children sin is anything they think, say, or do that displeases God. My thoughts, words and actions most often do not reflect a godly nature. Especially on the frustrating days, and there seems to be more of those than not.

Brotherly affection is one that I need to remember to extend in most areas outside of my home. It's important my choices as a mother are not used to judge other mothers for their choices that are different than my own.

Finally, there is love. I will admit, there are days I behave in many ways, but loving is not one of them. As a mother, the first and foremost prayer on my mind should be that God fills me with His unmatchable love.

Ruth Graham, Billy Graham's daughter, gave her testimony about leaving her husband of only five weeks. She said her father welcomed her home with loving arms, revealing to her the love of the Father. So often our kids need that prodigal son kind of love. They need a patient kind of love. Many days I recognize my attitude is lacking in the virtuous department and I can hear the strains of stress tromping through my house before I step foot out of bed. It's on those mornings I need more than ever to pray,

"Jesus, give me the love I need to love these children like the precious treasures that they are. Increase in me all these qualities I lack, from godliness to self-control when it comes to teaching my kids and loving them, so that my works may be fruitful, increasing the Kingdom, one child at a time, for your glory. Amen"

The Older Woman

THAT PAUL GUY was sometimes a little harsh, no, a lot harsh. He is hard to understand, and if he lived today he'd be the first one called a hateful, intolerant, bigot. He could step on toes and confuse the tar out of us with some of what he wrote to the Body of Christ. However, it didn't matter what he said, he hit the nail every time.

Lately I've been reminded of one of his most forgotten instructions to the church, it is the relationship between the generations.

"Older women likewise are to be reverent in behavior, not slanderers or slaves to much wine. They are to teach what is good, and so train the young women to love their husbands and children, to be self-controlled pure, working at home, kind and submissive to their own husbands that the word of God may not be reviled." Titus 2:3-5

I never fully understood how important this is in my own life, as a wife and a mother, until I couldn't find that older woman that encouraged me. Not that I didn't have any in my life that weren't Godly and encouraging, but we each have a soul sister personality that just vibes with our own.

I found myself in a place where I was the older woman, having been married longer, a mother longer, or just simply a Christian longer. I found myself in the role of a mentor and without a mentor of my own. It was a difficult season in my life because I felt like I was continually pouring out of my spirit with very little poured in from other women. I was the encourager to the discouraged mother. I was the loving wife to the wife struggling to love her husband. On my bad days, I only had one place to turn to be encouraged, renewed and filled up: prayer.

God always wants us to come to Him first. I had embraced a habit of running to my ladies, complaining and seeking their validation in my decisions or my anger, or their compliments when I felt down. God brought me to a dry season to remember at every difficult obstacle and every joyous celebration, His throne is my first stop.

That season also served a secondary purpose. I learned the importance of the wisdom of Godly women that have gone before me. Their comfort and prayers and hugs and smiles are invaluable and unrivaled.

God placed those Titus-2 women back in my life and their presence, their love, their hugs, words, prayers, and even the smile that appeared when I walked through the door, were like a fresh drink of water in the middle of a dry desert.

Enjoy those women that are your peers, and in the same stage of life as you. You need them and their friendship. But revel in the presence of the reverent older woman. Reverent is the key word here.

Paul told them to find the women who meet a list of criteria. First, they love God. Oh how they love Jesus, and it shows all over their lives.

These women don't gossip or slander other women. They edify and encourage other women! Don't become the kind of woman that rips apart other struggling mothers and wives to make yourself feel better about yourself.

They teach what is good, that is God's Word and his statutes, not worldly advice which leads you away from God.

They will encourage you to love your husbands and your children. Their advice will never encourage you to continue in anger or advise you to set yourself against your husband, but to pray for him and to trust in God to work in his heart too.

The reverent woman will not just display self-control, but spur you on to be self-controlled as well. She will never give you permission to indulge in sin. She will not give you trashy books to read which could result in dissatisfaction with your own marriage and husband, but she will encourage you to be pure in your mind and heart. The reverent woman works in her home and doesn't abandon it to chaos. She is kind to her family and to others, and then there is dreaded word "submissive." A good husband and wife know submission is mutual. Husbands were commanded to love their wives like Christ loves the Church, and what did Christ do for the Church He submitted himself to God to the point of death. In response to Christ's submission for her salvation, as a church we fully submit our lives to him. This is the picture of marriage. The reverent woman submits herself to her husband, not to be ruled over, but to honor and respect him as her husband.

Most of all, a reverent woman encourages you to honor the word of God, not revile it. She pours it in your heart, through her prayers and her words.

Never take for granted the value of a reverent older woman, full of not just knowledge, but experience as well. She's wanted to choke her husband on more occasions than you. She's felt the depth of the pain of knowing she doesn't deserve her husband's love and adoration. She has known the hours on her knees, praying for a husband that struggles at work or chooses to wander from God, and children that struggle with friends or choose rebellious behavior over the heart of God. She has. She will. She sees you wander into church with circles under your eyes, wrangling a toddler and a hyper preschooler, remembering fondly the days she was you. She has endured through hours of school work so that her child may learn. She knows the endless, sleepless nights with sick kids, cleaning up throw-up or praying your croupy baby will just be able to take one good breath. She knows the joy and the pain of marriage and children, church and work. She has and she knows sometimes submission feels impossible. Straying from purity has been a temptation. She has prayed to find her self-control, and she most likely has lost it and suffered the consequences. Find her and love her and appreciate all she has to offer. Even when it's not requested from her, let it be welcome.

Daily Surprises

SOME DAYS ARE just difficult. Some seasons are difficult. Then there are those days it seems my kids finally find a groove and do all they should do in a reasonable amount of time.

Then there are days like today, which is in all actuality the same as the last few weeks: long. It is after three pm and I still have two kids working on their school work, which means I am sitting right here beside them, babysitting them. I have asked myself if I am giving them too much work to accomplish in a reasonable amount of time, but I don't believe I am.

They are fun kids. Whereas my oldest wakes up around seven am, cooks his breakfast, and then proceeds with his school work until it is all finished, these two are more like Thing One and Thing Two. Distractions are abundant in the form of nerf guns, Legos, siblings, stuffed animals, food, and most recently, slime. I feel as though I need a vault where all distractions stay locked away until the proper time.

My daughter is the kind of child that leaves a trail of messes everywhere she goes. Her biggest problem begins when I ask her to pick up one mess, and along the way she makes a completely new mess of some sort, so we spend an infinite amount of time just trying to keep her stuff picked up, never actually accomplishing anything but picking up and messing up simultaneously.

While I sit next to these two, verbally gluing their bottoms to their seats and their lips shut, hoping I will be free of this prison they have created sooner rather than later in order to have a few minutes before I begin my next job as preparer of dinner food and chauffeuring children to extracurricular activities, I wonder if this is how God feels about me sometimes.

I spend most of my day distracted from the one thing that matters most, my time with the Father. My Bible sits next to me beckoning, yet I allow so much more to take precedence in my life over all my other jobs. It's always, "as soon as I get this load of laundry, I will spend some time in study and prayer." Or, "I'll get the kids busy on their work and then do mine." However, as a mother, we all know too well there is always something or someone waiting to be taken care of. That's why it's imperative I take the time. Most issues with children can wait, chores will wait, to-do lists will wait. It's funny how I never miss a shower or brushing my teeth because I have some job to do. I never miss breakfast or lunch. How much more important is the task of feeding my soul, washing my heart clean, and speaking with my Father, relying on His help and wisdom. Yet, regularly, I pass it over for less important tasks.

Distractions

I know your works, your toil and your patient endurance, and how you cannot bear with those who are evil, but have tested those who call themselves apostles and are not, and found them to be false. I know you are enduring patiently and bearing up for My Name's sake and you have not grown weary. But I have this against you, that you have abandoned the love you had at first.

Revelations 2:3-4

TODAY IS A day of distractions in this little school house. Due to a massive hail storm a few months ago, we have five or six vehicles parked outside our home and about the same amount of men on our roof scraping and banging as they put on a new roof. Needless to say, all the banging and crashing and pounding makes it difficult for even the most focused teacher to teach and kid to work. My six-year-old did more rolling around on the floor than reading today.

I considered giving up and taking a day off, but I know every day we take off is an extra day we must work in the end. I want to finish and not drag the school year out. So, we push through the noise and the activity and work in spite of it.

Surprisingly, my kids finished their work at a decent hour despite the distraction. I believe it was because I didn't let up as their teacher. I kept the "why" and the ultimate goal in mind and pushed them forward, patiently enduring the distraction not growing weary of our work. Now their reward is a coke date with dad.

Sometimes I feel as a Christian distractions in life take my focus off my "why" and my goal.

When hard times, sins, desires for worldly possessions, accomplishments, or fear of the future distract me from my walk, I don't always push through like we did today. However, focusing on my own righteous behavior and all I do right, can be the worst distraction of all.

God addressed the church in Ephesus in this verse in Revelations. He recognized how they had endured, persevered and pushed through the distractions. God could see all they had done right. However, even in enduring, they had forgotten their "why" and ultimately, their end goal: that is their first love, Jesus Christ and his love for people.

The day I became I believer in Jesus, I promised to share the good news of what He had done for me with whomever would listen. I wanted to take as many people to heaven with me as possible. Yet, many days I turn my eyes down and avoid even eye contact with those around me. I forget my "why". I forget my First Love. I forget my end goal!

I can speak out against heresy and false testimonies. I can stand against oppression and all kinds of evil and wickedness, but if I don't have love for the lost and the hurting all around me, I'm useless. Our first love is, and always should be, Jesus, but our love for other people go hand in hand with our love for Christ. We cannot love God, and not love the world. Loving God means loving people too!

I'm reminded today to avoid the worst distraction of all in my walk, that is religion without love. The worst distraction of all is to become wrapped up in my actions and my behavior, while forgetting Jesus is the reason why.

I pray, for myself and for you, to have our love for God and our love for people restored to its original passion and zealousness which existed in the beginning, while we strive to live a godly and virtuous life, we never forget the key to it all is love.

For Further study:
   1 Corinthians 13, 1 John 4:7-8

Nourishment

MY BIGGEST STRUGGLE as a stay at home mom is nourishing my body consistently, that means eating right. It seems silly when my job is to care for a home, plan and prepare meals for seven people, and educate five soon-to-be adults, but it's true. Every day when lunch-time rolls around, I struggle to eat. Not because I'm not hungry. I am. Today my stomach is letting me know I am short on fuel. However, nothing ever sounds good to me except junk food. I could eat a cinnamon roll and ice cream for lunch every single day. I rarely have leftovers with teenage boys in the house and salads just don't satisfy every single day. Sandwiches get old.

Despite my distaste for all that is in my refrigerator and pantry, my stomach speaks loudly that it is time for an intervention.

I am hungry, but here I sit, unable to make a decision on what I should eat.
Soon, my blood sugar will plummet, and I will find myself in a hypoglycemic state, too tired to function, or just simply grumpy. The entire scenario will end with a nap or junk food or both.

However, the longer I go, the more I sabotage, not just myself, my health, and my mood, but I sabotage our happy family homeostasis because we all know a grumpy mama means a grumpy household.

The same problems arise when I'm not feeding myself spiritually. When I do not fill myself up with God's word and His spirit, I sabotage every part of who I am, including my family. Today is one of those days where I am running off of yesterday's reserves of Bible study and prayer, but I can feel my spirit running low. My patience is running out. My energy level is declining. My frustration as I tell each of my kids 10 different times to go finish their school work builds more and more. The messes annoy me more. The arguing exasperates me. I know eventually I will hit bottom and I will crash.

The destruction of my happy, joy-filled, positive attitude is imminent, unless I intervene.

Jesus knew this to be true of himself as He walked this earth, and also true of his disciples and followers as well.

But now even more the report about him went abroad, and great crowds gathered to hear him and to be healed of their infirmities. But he

would withdraw to desolate places and pray.
Luke 5:16

As a mother and a wife, sometimes it feels as if the crowds are pressing in on me. Some moments all five of my children need my attention at the same time while I am in the middle of an important task. The pressure becomes unbearable. It feels suffocating at times. There are times my to-do list alone feels like a weight placed on my chest made to choke the life out of me.

Jesus gave us the perfect example. He knew He and his disciples needed the respite to commune with God and be renewed in order to meet the needs of the crowd. Likewise, we need the renewal of prayer and communion with God to be able to meet the needs of our family. Sometimes I feel guilty for taking the time to be alone, feeling as though I am neglecting my family. Jesus gave us an example to follow essential to our ministry as mothers and wives. It's one little sentence in the middle of all his activities, He withdrew. It seems insignificant in light of all the miracles He performed, but yet, there it sits, waiting to be noticed.

Jesus calming the storm in Mark 4:35-41 is my favorite example of Jesus' respite. Jesus went to the belly of the boat to sleep. He didn't leave his friends to pray, but to rest.

He slept through a storm so bad the disciples, men who lived and worked on the water and no doubt had seen plenty of storms in their life, thought they were going to die.

I'm from Oklahoma. We've had our share of storms and tornadoes, and never once did I tell my family I would be napping as in rolled one of those threats. Jesus did though.

In fact, it is in the crises, especially as mothers, we feel the need to be on high alert and skip any form of rest, but Jesus showed us a completely different example. He rested. He could rest because He knew who controlled the storm. *Why are you so afraid? Have you still no faith? Mark 4:40*

Our jobs as mothers and wives is physically, mentally, and oh so emotionally demanding, and without a respite to pray and refuel ourselves with the Spirit, and especially time to physically rest, we will run ourselves dry.

Father, as my spirit weakens, my stomach growls, and the pressures of motherhood press in on me, crowding out the Your voice, give me the opportunity to escape to some quiet place to pray. When my body is physically exhausted, give me the time to rest, even in the times of crisis, knowing You, Jesus, have authority over all

my storms, and You will stand guard over
me as I rest.

The Finish Line

AS I FINISH up this devotional, reading it over for corrections and edits, one thing stands out most to me; homeschooling is not the cause of my difficulties or troubles. It's life and all that encircles us outside our safe little home. Don't misunderstand, the kids and school cause plenty of stress. The teenage attitudes and complaining, six-year-old whining, little girl bossing, half finished worksheets and failed tests make me crazy too, but they are not the bulk of my stress. I'd be more calm and patient with those issues if bills or the broken vehicle wasn't weighing heavy on my mind in the midst of it all. I'd be less grumpy without my health issues flaring and causing me pain and discomfort. I'd have more energy to run my home with a joyful heart if those I love weren't suffering, or I hadn't said one thing to one person and upset them.

My kids are not my problem, neither is the responsibility of their education, and they are not the part of my life that causes me the most stress. If anything, they bring me far more joy than stress, however, they bear the brunt of all of my outside stress.

I read a quote the other day that made an interesting observation. Stress is not caused by your circumstances, but rather by your reaction to your circumstances. A change of attitude most often can relieve a huge amount of stress.

One great example is something I learned while fighting with my husband. I hold grudges. It takes me days to stop being angry and allow him to love me again. Holding on to anger and bitterness for days caused so much stress for me, so I changed the way I thought about him. I asked myself, is it worth it to be angry and send him off to work like this, risking regret the rest of my life? If he died today and this was our last day together, how would that make me feel? At those questions I found the courage to swallow my pride and kiss him goodbye with a heartfelt, "I love you." Simply by changing my attitude and my perspective, turning my concentration from myself and my own hurt to the one I love the most on this planet and his needs, I changed my heart too. My attitude leads my heart and my mind.

There is no magic wand I can wave that will take away all the pressures of this life and make raising my kids a constant joy. Reading over the different ways God spoke to me this school year made me realize it is in all those difficult times, the times when I need a gallon of coffee just to start my day, that my children keep me in line. I wake up with a purpose and a goal because of those kids, and sometimes it is in fulfilling that goal I escape the difficulties in life and find joy in my day.

Honestly, today as I edited for hours on end with an interruption every two minutes, I found myself increasingly annoyed by the silly little interruptions and frustrated at my kids. Staying on top of laundry, editing my feeble attempt at sharing God's Word with the world, teaching five kids out of the side of my mouth, and making sure the dog stays off the furniture meant I had no time for the silly questions or especially, making decisions concerning video games and walks to the store. That's when my six year-old asked, "Mommy, will you jump on the trampoline with me?" In my head the answer was obvious. "No. I don't have time for that! I still have three loads of laundry, sheets to put on the bed, forty pages to edit, and the kitchen to clean before I can start dinner to have it finished in time for your brother to take something to eat to work with him. Go find someone else to play with."

BUT.!

Yep. That word came up again.

But God gave me this little one. I never once had a day I wished my kids were gone. In fact, since I started writing these devotionals, my oldest has started his first job and now works three nights a week, and I miss him at our dinner table. My two and three boys have started volunteering on

Friday afternoons, and once again I miss their presence and their incessant questions.

Of all the difficult days and even with all their difficult behaviors, my kids have been my joy, the source of my comfort, and my reminder to take a deep breath in the midst of all the mess and enjoy them, while they are still here. Have you ever been super stressed, angry, sad, or frustrated and in the midst of those negative feelings, sat down to rock a baby to sleep? There is no greater stress relief than holding a baby. They truly are God's gift and His greatest blessing. I miss those afternoons rocking a baby, slowing down physically and mentally, and meditating on the awe wrapped up in the creation of one tiny human being.

I can't rock him to sleep anymore so I put the computer aside and jumped on the trampoline. We laughed and played, and my spirit was renewed and no longer exasperated by my long to-do list.

It is our privilege and joy to stay home and educate our children, because they are our reward for the sacrifices we make. They are the reward for all the other pressures this world heaps upon our shoulders. They bring a smile in the midst of sadness, playfulness in the midst of tireless work, laughter in the midst of exhaustion, wisdom in the simplest form, accountability in our bad behavior, and riches where we go without.

This, dear Mama, is why you do it. This is why day after day, you put on your big girl pants, pretend you are brave enough to face the little circus you created, push the covers back and emerge to face another day as a teacher, nurse, counselor, chauffeur, cook, laundress, maid, personal stylist, financier, personal shopper, party planner, physical therapist, coach and… well, you get the point. This could go on all day. The work is worth the reward. It is the most difficult work there is in the world and that is why we need more help, the kind which can only come from leaning on Jesus every moment of every day, and of course, coffee helps too.